T0328699

Cambridge Elements ≡

Cambridge Elements in International Economics
edited by
Kenneth A. Reinert
George Mason University

VIRTUAL TRADE IN A CHANGING WORLD

Comparative Advantage, Growth and Inequality

Sugata Marjit
Hong Kong Polytechnic University and Indian Institute of Foreign Trade

Gouranga G. Das
Hanyang University

Biswajit Mandal
Visva-Bharati University

CAMBRIDGE
UNIVERSITY PRESS

CAMBRIDGE
UNIVERSITY PRESS

Shaftesbury Road, Cambridge CB2 8EA, United Kingdom

One Liberty Plaza, 20th Floor, New York, NY 10006, USA

477 Williamstown Road, Port Melbourne, VIC 3207, Australia

314–321, 3rd Floor, Plot 3, Splendor Forum, Jasola District Centre, New Delhi – 110025, India

103 Penang Road, #05–06/07, Visioncrest Commercial, Singapore 238467

Cambridge University Press is part of Cambridge University Press & Assessment, a department of the University of Cambridge.

We share the University's mission to contribute to society through the pursuit of education, learning and research at the highest international levels of excellence.

www.cambridge.org
Information on this title: www.cambridge.org/9781009101332

DOI: 10.1017/9781009105743

First published 2023

A catalogue record for this publication is available from the British Library.

ISBN 978-1-009-10133-2 Paperback
ISSN 2631-8598 (online)
ISSN 2631-858X (print)

Virtual Trade in a Changing World

Comparative Advantage, Growth and Inequality

Cambridge Elements in International Economics

DOI: 10.1017/9781009105743
First published online: August 2023

Sugata Marjit
Hong Kong Polytechnic University and Indian Institute of Foreign Trade

Gouranga G. Das
Hanyang University

Biswajit Mandal
Visva-Bharati University

Author for correspondence: Sugata Marjit, marjit@gmail.com

Abstract: Virtual economic transactions have radically transformed the way we think about trade and markets in closed and open economies. Due to the continuous decline in the costs of both information and communications and setting up a phenomenally large number of virtual platforms, the importance of "time" as an essential element in the discourse on international trade can in no way be set aside. This work delves deep into the issue of how time enters as a major catalyst of international trade and virtual transactions. This changes the way we look at ideas of comparative advantage, factor mobility, growth, income distribution and allied concepts. A key result is that greater physical distance might encourage trade, contrary to what we are accustomed to accepting.

Keywords: trade, time zone differences, trade in business services, skilled and unskilled labor, day-shift and night-shift work

ISBNs: 9781009101332 (PB), 9781009105743 (OC)
ISSNs: 2631-8598 (online), 2631-858X (print)

Contents

Preface

The emergence of information and communication technology (ICT)-enabled production networks and e-commerce has revolutionized global transactions and reshaped the nature of international trade. And while no one can ignore the global scale of virtual platforms like Facebook, Amazon, Netflix and Google (collectively, FANG), organizing production virtually is another aspect of global trade. So far, the pure theory of international trade – the traditional workhorse models – has not incorporated this aspect into an analytically tractable framework. This Element fills this gap by exploring the role of time in production over geographically separated regions. In other words, we go beyond the traditional corpus of trade theory literature – which emphasizes the roles of factor endowments, technology, and preferences for commodities – to look at how the natural geographical location of a trade partner across non-overlapping time zones could be a source of comparative advantage and even enable work to take place continuously across the full spectrum of twenty-four hours. If companies can overcome the obstacle of distance, it could generate growth via virtual trade and create a truly global value chain with interlinked production networks. Virtual trade (VT) opens windows of opportunity for organizing production globally. In such models, VT automatically leads to faster growth by increasing global productivity without the requirement of bringing in additional structural changes. The conventional trade and growth literature emphasizes the roles of research and development, innovation, and product heterogeneities, along with resource endowments and technologies, but it does not much attend to organizing production virtually, which further enhances economic growth through use of ICT-enabled production networks. However, VT also opens the door for rising inequality as trade, productivity growth and inequality go hand in hand. This Element itself is the product of the virtual exchange of ideas between India and South Korea; we took advantage of the time difference between these countries during the several stages of research and work that went into writing it, and benefited immensely from virtual communication and stimulating interactions via numerous seminars and webinars, despite the social distancing prohibitions under the long spell of the COVID-19 pandemic. Given the fact that the menace is not yet over at the time of writing this Element, the importance of VT can in no way be overlooked.

This Element brings trade, time and distance together for the first time to explain the stylized facts and evidence of overwhelming patterns of trade in ICT-enabled services where virtual exchange leads to gains from trade and growth. For example, by using variants or extensions of the elementary Ricardian and Heckscher–Ohlin–Samuelson models, this Element shows that such trade is welfare-enhancing as it stimulates higher trade volumes, lower prices, and growth with differential factor returns. Its attention to division of labor by time zones is the crucial aspect that makes this Element unique. Thus, it adds 'time' as the fourth dimension of trade at the rudimentary level, opening up and offering insights into a new vista of research in the subdiscipline of pure theory of international trade. Our sincere belief is that readers of all genres will find it extremely useful for its novelty of exposition and its extension of neoclassical trade theory beyond typical textbook fashion.

1 Introduction

"We must use time as a tool, not as a couch."
John F. Kennedy[1]

1.1 Virtual Trade and Related Issues: Basic Concepts and Point of Departure

Time is our greatest resource, without doubt. The quote that opens this section signifies that time can be "buckled" to bridge the distance between time zones (henceforth, TZs) so as to execute actions faster. It can also be utilized as a "tool" for doing something quickly, to one's own "natural" advantage, rather than losing the opportunity to work more during the saved time. The opportunity cost of *losing time* is high when technological boons via information and communication technology (ICT) have spread their wings everywhere.[2] This perspective underlies this Element where we show how we can reap the benefits of organizing production stages utilizing TZ differences across geographically separated regions, thereby increasing productivity, growth and welfare. We focus and extensively highlight an idea that hails from the Ricardian story of comparative advantage and brings in time as a catalyst of international trade that is independent of all factors, as has been discussed in the literature to date. This visualization of trade theory is fourth in line after the Ricardian, Heckscher–Ohlin–Samuelson (HOS) and Dixit-Stiglitz-Krugman trade models. Moreover, it shows that countries that are identical in terms of preference, endowments and technology may trade if they are located in separated TZs. This very Element is the product of *virtual exchange of ideas* among the authors; three authors communicated across semi-overlapping TZs (between Seoul in South Korea and Kolkata in India, with a three-and-a-half-hour time gap) to take advantage of zero communication costs, to simultaneously interact (real-time interaction with short time gaps) and share work. We realized that *if* they had been nonoverlapping time zones (henceforth, NOLTZs), the frequency of the real-time interaction would have been less but the virtual trade (henceforth, VT) in ideas would have been at least the same, or more intense.[3]

---

[1] From John F. Kennedy's address to the National Association of Manufacturers, in New York City, December 5, 1961 (www.jfklibrary.org).

[2] The benefits of ICT as a general-purpose technology ushering in the third industrial revolution can in no way be exaggerated because of its omnipresence in every sphere of life. Advanced technologies due to chain reactions of ICT spillovers (e.g., mobile apps) have played a facilitating role for paperless trade and business processes, transactions of goods and services, logistics management, customs e-declarations, even transparency and visibility.

[3] In completely overlapping TZs (say Japan and South Korea), utilizing TZ differences plays a diminished role, although virtual interactions for business services could still happen depending

Also, given the COVID-19 outbreak and the norms of social distancing, no other time is as ripe as this for writing about "virtual exchange"; the pandemic has shaken the world, hindering typical market transactions in physical proximity. The containment measures for avoiding contact-intensity have led to disruptions of activities (Bonadio et al. [2021], Marjit and Das [2021]) with separation of economic agents. Pandemic-led trade restrictions (internal as well as external) have curtailed flows of goods and flows of people, forcing us to continue with necessary economic transactions *without* the physical presence of suppliers and demanders at the same point in time. Also, fear about the backlash on globalization and disruption of production networks based on fragmented stages has loomed large. This has led to the flourishing of the virtual market. Delivery costs being low, virtual transactions have gained pace using the communications network, with ICT facilitating the exchanges. This has minimized, to some extent, the risk of trade disruptions and, in a wider sense, apprehension about "deglobalization" (Bonadio et al. [2021], World Bank [2020, 2021]).

Briefly, all these imply that geographical distance is related to TZ.[4] Exploiting TZs directly raises production levels of goods and services, trade volume in general and, specifically, cross-TZ VT in intermediate or final (labor) services. This, in turn, leads to capital accumulation (as output increases) and productivity growth affecting all the participants linked in a virtual platform. Such a trade is gainful and welfare-augmenting as consumers get access to products much earlier (delivery timeliness matters) than without offshoring possibilities under virtual exchanges. Availability of global high-bandwidth telecom infrastructure catalyzes cost reduction via offshoring and ensures timely delivery of products. Business-services[5] trade takes advantage of NOLTZs as the emergence of ICT implies *nonrequirement* of both the physical presence of buyers and sellers at the point of transaction and physical transshipment, rendering shipment cost negligible (see Marjit, Mandal and Nakanishi [2020], ch. 6). Thus, utilizing TZ differences circumvents "delaying cost" (like shipment costs in the conventional sense) and reduces the iceberg effect; consequently, transportation

---

on the nature of the services and activities. In other words, TZ difference plays a less important role the higher is the degree of the trade partners' overlapping time, although VT could be large.

[4] Different measures of TZ are distance in nautical miles between capital cities, or hours between capitals, geographical centers, etc. This is also related to synchronization and continuity effects for coordinating fragmented tasks.

[5] Business services such as engineering, consulting, business process outsourcing (BPO), software development, etc. have emerged as the share of ICT in exports and imports has soared in the USA, India and almost every other nation.

becomes quicker and cheaper in a sense that guarantees timely production and consumption.[6]

In this Element, we discuss this point of departure from the traditional modes of international trade based on three dimensions, namely, differences in technology (productivity), resource endowments, and diversity of tastes and preferences for differentiated products. We then add a *fourth dimension, TZ differences*, where two nations (identical or nonidentical) located in two NOLTZs (say USA vis-à-vis Japan or India or South Korea) can use a virtual communication network to participate in gainful trade. This is *VT*, defined as transactions that don't involve the physical transfer of goods and services. Thus, by taking advantage of separated TZs, countries can engage in trade via global division of labor on a virtual platform. This involves trade in intermediate or final services (essentially labor services or tasks) dispersed across countries in separated TZs and, in the process, reduces untimely delivery of final goods and services when consumers value time-cost of consumption in their preference structure. Thus, *TZ factor* is the additional determinant, or *fourth dimension*, underlying trade in services.

As we know even from standard texts (for example, Feenstra and Taylor [2021], Krugman, Obstfeld and Melitz [2018]), distance as a "natural" trade barrier has already gained the attention of trade theorists. The main focus of gravity models has been on the role of physical distance and proxies for the critical role of "trade frictions" as trade impediments; these models have also dealt at length with the role of trade costs and the pecuniary transaction costs inhibiting trade volumes between countries (Anderson and van Wincoop [2004], Chaney [2011], Head and Mayer [2014]). The rise in e-commerce and e-business that has come about since the signing of the World Trade Organization's (WTO) Information Technology Agreement (ITA) has led to *trade facilitation* measures. However, the "distance puzzle," also referred to as the "missing globalization puzzle," has been occupying researchers' attention. Although "distance elasticity" in gravity estimates hovered around −1, recent research finds that distance elasticity has fallen (despite cross-country heterogeneity) for major high- and middle-income countries that has been positively affected by globalization of trade (Borchert and Yotov [2017], Sun [2021]). We can attribute this to several factors such as fragmentation of production, changing merchandise export structures, the share of ICT and high-tech goods in export bundles, foreign direct investment (FDI) inflows and offshore

---

[6] Iceberg-type transaction cost is common in gravity models where a fraction of the good is lost during transit (say, rotten perishable products) so that less than the original shipment arrives at the destination. With communication networks, such an iceberg effect diminishes due to time-saving technical changes (quicker delivery with lower cost).

outsourcing between countries, even those that are not so far apart (Das and Han [2013], Feenstra [1998, 2010], Jones and Kierzkowski [2001], World Bank [2020, 2021]). This is *without worrying* about the TZ-related *"natural" comparative advantage* of agents located in geographically separated places with distinct time differences.

The most important thing to note is that this type of virtual transaction began taking place a long time ago as the necessity of the supplier being physically present and tangible goods and services being shipped was reduced thanks to the ICT-led broadband innovation network (see Acemoglu, Ozdaglar and Tahbaz-Saleh [2010], Chaney [2011], Kikuchi [2011], Malgouyres, Mayer and Mazet-Sonilhac [2021], Marjit, Mandal and Nakanishi [2020]). This caused a sea change in the way production and international trade take place, and led to the emergence of a *new paradigm* of production – taking advantage of shift-working during only the daytime hours of the participating countries – and an abrupt increase in trade volumes among countries in NOLTZs. Thus, exploiting TZ differences based on the day–night cycle of production and services trade via usage of ICT-enabled services, unlike what gravity models predict, speeds up global integration and growth based on sheer "complementary" natural comparative advantage.

What is important to note at this point is that both nations can take advantage of this natural endowment of geographical or longitudinal difference causing the day–night cycle, and workers even with similar productivity levels can share the workload in the value-chain by making the production run on a twenty-four-hour cycle. Thus, unlike conventional models of trade based on asymmetries in terms of labor productivity, resources, demands and product varieties, here trade can occur between two otherwise symmetrical or asymmetric nations based only on locations in *naturally endowed* TZs. With the ICT-led technological breakthroughs that started emerging from the latter half of the twentieth century (and currently the fourth industrial revolution encompassing artificial intelligence [AI], automation, etc.), communication costs nosedived. For example, Osnago and Tan (2016) have shown that a 10 percent increase in internet adoption by exporters leads to a 1.9 percent increase in bilateral exports, while a 10 percent increase in ICT adoption by importers causes a 0.6 percent increase in the average value of existing exports. See Figures 1 and 2.

Globally, digitally deliverable services accelerated from below 52 percent of services exports in 2019 to about 64 percent in 2020, while ICT services grew from 10 percent to almost 14 percent. Changes in the composition of trade – that is, the emergence of intangible services and offshoring activities – that exploit NOLTZ differences counter the negative effects of physical distance per se and

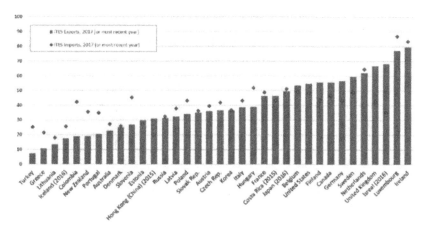

Figure 1 Potential IT-enabled services (ITES) as a percentage of total trade in services.

Source: Organisation for Economic Co-operation and Development (OECD) Trade in Services EBOPS 2010, which is a database showing international trade in services by partner economy (https://doi.org/10.1787/ca7a6d85-en), and International Monetary Fund (IMF) balance of payments (BOP) statistics (https://data.imf.org/?sk=7A51304B-6426-40C0-83DD-CA473CA1FD52).

Note: Potential ITES refers to services categories that can predominantly be delivered digitally (see also Section 4).

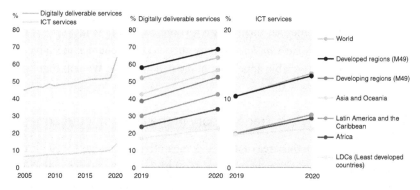

Figure 2 Rise in digital virtual trade in services.

Source: United Nations Conference on Trade and Development (UNCTAD) digital economy statistics (unctadstat.unctad.org).

lead to more transactions, resulting in welfare gains. It is obvious that maximum VT could take place across countries located in NOLTZs, while physical goods trade could flourish among those located in overlapping time zones (OLTZs) due to the transportation cost effects of relative proximity. It being possible to

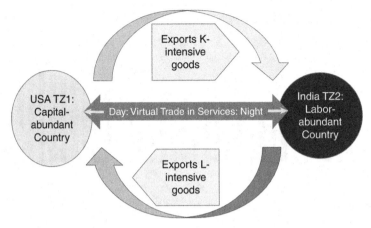

Figure 3 Conceptual framework for virtual trade based on time zone.

economize on "time-costs" due to the bandwidth of the ICT networks is the tour de force behind such economic exchange. Unlike the traditional corpus of trade theory where distance deters trade, here distance promotes trade; enabled by ICT, companies can perform seamlessly online, providing combinations of specialized tasks and services over asymmetric TZs. Figure 3 offers a schematic presentation where TZ2 and TZ1 can be used interchangeably for day and night.

Table 1 cogently presents the comparative perspectives of the literature on conventional trade and on trade over virtual platforms, to highlight the point of departure.[7]

It is important to note that incorporating volume of trade with "TZ" as the variable in the *otherwise standard* gravity model could counter the adverse effect of the distance variable appearing in the denominator. We will highlight such things in Sections 3 and 5.

1.2 Literature Review: Trade Theory in the Light of Time Zones

Substantial research in this area of natural comparative advantage-based virtual exchange has come up with new insights. Most of the papers incorporating TZ differences in international trade are theoretical in nature: some deal with a competitive framework and others are based on imperfectly competitive market characteristics. Here, we provide a synoptic overview of the most significant contributions within a cogent analytical framework.

The importance of communication networks in TZ-related services trade is aptly described in Kikuchi (2011), where exploiting the technological

---

[7] We do not exhaustively present the variants, such as Dornbusch et al. (1977), Marjit (1987) and Sanyal (1983), that are based on these core ones.

Table 1 Schematic presentation of the different paradigms of modern trade theory

Paradigms	Theory and models	Sources of comparative advantage	Key ideas and assumptions	Patterns of specialization	Reference for genesis of ideas	Point of departure
Classical	Adam Smith's wealth of nations and absolute advantage theory	Absolute cost differences, TOT	Division of labor, specialization, scale economies	Specialization in activities with lowest absolute costs	Smith ([1776] 1976)	Mercantilism (protectionism)
Classical	David Ricardo's theory of comparative cost advantage	Differences in technology, labor productivity (differing unit labor requirement), demand has no role in this supply-side model	Labor theory of value, perfect competition, one factor, fixed coefficient technology, perfect mobility	Specialization in activities with lower comparative labor costs	Ricardo ([1817] 1951) and for Ricardo's views on foreign trade, see Jones and Weder (2019)	Relative cost differs

Table 1 (cont.)

Paradigms	Theory and models	Sources of comparative advantage	Key ideas and assumptions	Patterns of specialization	Reference for genesis of ideas	Point of departure
Neoclassical trade theory	HOS model and factor proportions	Differences in relative abundance of resource endowments, supply-side model, long-run factor mobility	Two factors of production but same technology, perfect mobility of factors, perfect competition, factor-intensity differences and nonreversal, same tastes and preferences, homothetic demand	Countries specialize in (and export) products that are relatively intensive in their abundant factors, and import those that are relatively intensive in their relatively scarce resources	Heckscher (1919); Ohlin (1933) This is couched in general equilibrium theory (Jones, 1965)	Resource-based, Rybczynski effect for factor endowment changes, Stolper–Samuelson effect for tariff or relative price changes (real wage vs. real returns to capital)

Neoclassical theory	Specific-factor (Ricardo–Viner) model	Short-run factor-specificity and resource endowments	Three-factors-two-goods model: two sector-specific immobile factors (e.g., land and capital) with one mobile factor (labor)	Countries specialize and trade in goods as in HOS, but distributional implications are significant for the factors	Jones (1971), Samuelson (1971)	Distributional implications of trade such as wage inequality etc.
New trade theory	Krugman (1979, 1980), Helpman (1981), Grubel–Lloyd index of intra-industry trade, etc.	Scale economies, size and location, product variety and love of variety, intra-industry trade, demand for characteristics	Increasing returns, economies of scale, agglomeration and geography, product differentiation, monopolistic competition, duopoly/oligopolistic model	Differentiated goods, demand plays a role	Dixit and Stiglitz (1977), Krugman (1979, 1980, 1983), Helpman (1981), Brander and Krugman (1980), etc.	Product differentiations, imperfect competition, love of variety

Table 1 (cont.)

Paradigms	Theory and models	Sources of comparative advantage	Key ideas and assumptions	Patterns of specialization	Reference for genesis of ideas	Point of departure
Hetero-geneous firm models/ "new" new trade theory	Melitz (2003), Antràs and Helpman (2004), Bernard et al. (2003)	Organizational choices of firms, trade costs, FDI, sourcing patterns	Intra-industry heterogeneity of producers	Imperfect competition, trade in tasks, incomplete contracts	Melitz (2003), Grossman and Rossi-Hansberg (2008), Melitz and Redding (2012)	Trade costs, trade–FDI relationship
Post-neoclassical neo-technology-based theories	Posner's technology trade gap, Vernon's product life cycle theory	Technology and innovation	Innovation and diffusion patterns	Developed nations specialize in new products and developing standardized ones	Vernon (1966), Posner (1973), Porter (1985), Grossman and Helpman (1990)	Life cycle of products

VT with TZ differences	NOLTZ					
	differences based on longitudinal distance (natural comparative advantage), delivery timeliness, consumer time-preference, skill, etc.	ICT-enabled business services, geographical separation, time-saving technical change, productivity growth, capital accumulation, technical advancement in ICT networks and growth	Introducing TZ differences in traditional workhorse of models, viz.., Ricardian, HOS, perfect competition, imperfect competition, heterogeneous firm model, with human capital	TZ exploitation, labor cost differences, task specialization, induced growth in partners via TOT effect, implications of factor prices (wage inequality), work-shifts in day–night cycle	Marjit (2007), Kikuchi (2011), Marjit, Mandal and Nakanishi (2020), Kikuchi and Long (2011), Kikuchi, Marjit and Mandal (2013)	Fourth dimension, ICT as major underlying catalyst, labor allocation between day and night shifts, wage differentials between shifts

advancements in interconnected communication networks is shown to increase the connectivity of services firms and improve the terms of trade (TOT), with gains from interconnections with other countries. The idea of TZ differences in a trade model was first spelled out in Marjit (2007) in a Ricardian framework where the possibility of trade between countries in different TZs was modeled with clear implications for gainful trade. The effects of trade between countries located in different TZs on the factor market and the factor prices of the trading countries have been examined in Kikuchi and Long (2011), Kikuchi and Marjit (2010), Kikuchi, Marjit and Mandal (2013), Matsuoka and Fukushima (2010), and Nakanishi and Long (2015).

This type of trade becomes possible only through the availability of a well-functioning information communication network. As mentioned in Section 1.1, such a network allows *fragmenting* the production of a service to countries located in NOLTZs. In a sense, this idea is quite similar to the idea of vertical specialization, with intermediate inputs being produced in different stages before being assembled to produce the final good. Additionally, fragmented production together with use of different NOLTZs allows a production process to operate continuously for twenty-four hours as the end of one country's working hours marks the beginning of the other country's workday. Communication networks primarily link different users and allow them to share information. Recent developments in telecommunications networks have made services more tradable both within and between countries. Kikuchi (2011) explores such aspects of communication networks in terms of gains from trade.

Depending on the magnitude of offshoring and transportation costs, a firm chooses whether to undertake the entire production process at home or in the foreign country, or whether to offshore to the foreign country only those stages of production for which the offshoring cost is low. The phenomenon of lower price, especially lower labor cost, on the other hand, is nicely explained in Choi and Choi (2013) where lower labor cost encourages fragmentation of production to different countries. The uncertainty regarding the prevailing wage rates in the developing countries is also modeled. On the other hand, Hummels and Schaur (2013) point out how an air route is chosen instead of a sea route for delivering goods in the United States, even when air-shipping costs are higher. This is because trading goods via sea route takes more time. This in turn imposes significant costs, with pronounced impact when consumers change their product choices over time. Deardorff (2003) also explains the importance of time in the sphere of production and trade by emphasizing the fact that development in ICT can make production quicker. Hence, proper utilization of time helps to serve the consumer better in terms of both production and consumption because, in case of delayed delivery or production, inventory holding may or may not be useful for fulfilling product demand on time. What it boils down to is that using TZ differences paves the way for using the work-time (day, per se) available for production more judiciously, ensuring early delivery of products.

This idea – of using a communication network to outsource unfinished work to one or multiple trading partners – was first posited in Marjit (2007) in a simple Ricardian model with two countries, on the one hand, and the rest of the world (ROW), on the other. The key to it is the two countries utilizing the difference of their geographic locations and hence their nonoverlapping working hours. Kikuchi (2006) is another important contribution in this regard where a three-country model is used to show how utilizing TZ differences can influence the pattern of comparative advantage and affect the location decisions of firms. Kikuchi and Iwasa (2008) also address this, taking two countries (Home and Foreign) located in NOLTZs that differ in size in terms of labor endowment.

Based on the foundational arguments of TZ difference and trade, Kikuchi and Marjit (2010) elegantly point out how services trade across different TZs can be gainful when nighttime demand in one TZ is fulfilled by using daytime supply in another TZ. So, Kikuchi and Marjit (2010) indicates why international wage rate differentials can also be utilized along with daytime–nighttime wage differentials to induce trade. This kind of trade is termed in the literature as a new version of *periodic intra-industry trade*. On the other hand, taking two identical countries located in NOLTZs, two goods (one involving shift-working, the other not) and two factors (labor and capital), Kikuchi and Long (2011) demonstrate the impact of periodic intra-industry trade in labor services on the nature of shift-working, on factor prices and on the pattern of comparative advantage. Mandal, Marjit and Nakanishi (2015) is an interesting addition to this strand of literature. This work illustrates how reduced communication costs along with the presence of TZ differences affect prices and the inflow of educational capital, sector-specific labor and intersectorally mobile capital. Nevertheless, Nakanishi and Long (2015) also analyze the effect of trade on factor prices when the two countries Home and Foreign differ in size.

The potential link between trade and growth has received less attention in the standard trade literature. In relation to this connection, Kikuchi and Marjit (2011) propose a two-country model of intermediate services trade that captures the role of TZ difference in economic growth.[8] As in Kikuchi and Iwasa (2008), there are two countries, Home and Foreign, located in different TZs with nonoverlapping working hours. There are two sectors – the final good sector

---

[8] See Marjit, Mandal and Nakanishi (2020).

and the intermediate business-services sector. Domestic production of business services requires twenty-four working hours, which means that two consecutive calendar dates should be used to finish the task and the product is ready for sale after those two calendar dates. Therefore, the delivery of the domestic business services involves significant cost in terms of delay. To capture the positive time-cost for delivery of the intermediates, we need to consider the iceberg effect on the delivery cost. Kikuchi and Marjit (2011) consider a time-saving technological advancement in one of the countries and demonstrate that with a reduction in delivery cost in one country there is an increase in the marginal productivity of capital in both countries at the same rate, resulting in concomitant economic growth in *both* countries simultaneously.[9]

By considering a Cobb–Douglas production function with capital and an intermediate input, Mandal (2015), based on Kikuchi and Marjit (2010), examines the relationship among distance, production and trade in different TZs in relation to its impacts on welfare and economic growth. Similar to Marjit (2007), production of output requires two consecutive stages or workdays. Because of this, the service output cannot be delivered in a timely manner, reducing consumers' valuation of the good. This time-preference is denoted by a discount factor, as in Marjit (2007). Mandal (2015) relates time-preference to the distance between TZs. Analogously, Marjit and Mandal (2017) also demonstrate the positive impact on growth of two trading countries being engaged in VT.

Trade on virtual platforms may involve goods and services that are typically nontraded international but traded domestically, such as locally produced groceries and virtually ordered takeout dinners for home delivery. From a different angle, this also generates VT depending on who values their time more. Time as an element of leisure and consumption has been treated in economics over a considerable length of time. Both physical and virtual access to goods depends on the relative cost of time. Marjit and Yang (2021) show that poorer countries have a relative demand bias in favor of nonvirtual goods since low real wages and incomes imply a lower relative cost of time. They demand more nonvirtual goods (i.e., goods available in typical physical stores or outlets) that can be accessed physically, with close proximity of buyers and sellers. Given similar supply conditions, richer countries will import virtual goods over online platforms. Also, as consumption of nonvirtual goods involves time, increasing consumption of those goods involves increasing the time-cost and, hence, would eat into the gains from trade of the poorer countries. This alters the

---

[9] Das (2007) builds an applied general equilibrium north–south model to show the effect of using ICT spillover via human capital.

standard look of the well-known gains from trade theorem. Marjit, Pant and Huria (2020) argue that the incentive of saving the time-cost of household work induces skilled workers to outsource such work to unskilled labor who have a lower opportunity cost relative to time and that this really may have significant implications for wage inequality.

On the empirical front, Stein and Daude (2007) use OECD data for seventeen OECD source countries and fifty-eight host countries from 1997 to 1999 to find the effect of TZ difference on bilateral FDI. Hattari and Rajan (2008), in discussing the inflow of FDI to Asian regions, taking data from UNCTAD on FDI and transnational corporations (TNCs) and the Economist Intelligence Unit's (EIU) World Investment Service databases from 1990 to 2005, also show some similar results. Egger and Larch (2013), using the trade data of fifty-one US states and ten Canadian provinces, show a negative impact of TZ difference while estimating its impact on trade cost and trade in general equilibrium. Head, Mayer and Ries (2009) point out the growth of the services trade over the years, investigating the effects on the international services trade of both distance and TZ difference. They develop a model of bilateral services trade where the services positions of one country are filled, via communication networks, by workers based in other countries. Dettmer (2014) gives empirical evidence of a continuity effect, while estimating the impact of TZ difference on the business and commercial services trade and the merchandise trade. Tomasik (2013) also gives empirical evidence of both a synchronization and a continuity effect. For this purpose, OECD export data spanning 2000–8 for twenty source countries and fifty-six recipient countries are taken and analyzed. The outcome shows a negative impact of synchronization and a positive impact of continuity on goods and services exports.

1.3 Comparative Advantage, Growth and Inequality: Traditional and Emerging Issues

Growth itself is a *time-varying* process.[10] Depending on the parametric config-urations specific to each model (e.g., the savings or investment rate, rate of time-preference for consumption, rate of depreciation, level of human capital or skill, resource endowments, research and development (R&D) activity, nature of technical progress, technology transmission), the economy moves to a balanced growth path or steady state and achieves sustained growth. This has some impacts on the returns to factors. Analysis of modern economic growth has been challenging, with constant research flooding the field, spanning at least the last eighty years or so, and the emergence of a "new" growth theory

---

[10] On this, more detail in Section 3.2. Here we offer a snapshot view in the digital era.

(see Acemoglu [2009], Aghion and Durlauf [2005], Helpman [2004], Jones [2016], Lucas [2002], Sen [1960], and Solow [2000] for a comprehensive account).

With economic integration and the cascading effects of falling trade barriers, growth has spread via trade and FDI. Increasingly, countries have become intertwined. Globalization in the twentieth century can be viewed as happening in three waves: (i) 1870–1914 (seen as the first "golden age" thanks to falling transport and communication costs, the invention of the steam engine, electricity and telegraphy, and the liberal trade policy); (ii) 1945–80s (the second, post–World War II golden age due to multilateral trade liberalization along with containerization for transcontinental shipping of goods, communication satellites and jet planes); and (iii) 1980s–90s onwards (thanks to semi-conductors and microprocessors, the Internet, mobile communications, the emergence of ICT, the further decline in the costs of computing, communication, transportation and air cargo, and continued liberalization due to the General Agreement of Tariffs and Trade [GATT] and the WTO). See, for example, Baldwin (2016), Robertson (2003) and World Bank (2001), to name but three.

The most important thing to note is that in all these three phases, given the liberal trade policy "space," the common thread is the constantly evolving role of *technology as a time-saving force* stimulating trade and commerce. That said, the *TZ* aspect has never been explicitly analyzed as a "new" natural source of *comparative advantage* (see Sections 1.1 and 1.2). Therefore, other than focusing on conventional resource or labor productivity or scale economies-based comparative advantage, all the existing works on trade–growth linkages are deficient, failing to capture the *role of utilizing TZ gaps* in inducing economic growth. To understand the point of departure and the paradigmatic changes, we touch here upon the basics of the traditional focus. However, Section 3 elaborates more on this.

Conventionally, since the introduction of Adam Smith's ([1776] 1976) doctrine of absolute advantage and David Ricardo's ([1817] 1951) concept of comparative advantage, and down the path in the twentieth-century toward modern neoclassical trade theory, the role of trade as either an engine or a handmaiden of growth has spawned debates on both sides (Crafts [1973], Irwin [1996], Kravis [1970]). There have been arguments on the role of international trade in inducing growth (Bardhan [2003], Findlay [1984], Helpman [2004], Kemp and Shimomura [1999]). Most of the static models of trade, like the HOS and the specific-factor models that take resources and technology as given, seem quite incapable of handling the dynamic aspect of long-run growth, focusing instead primarily on the welfare and distributional aspects of gains from trade. Although Bernard et al. (2003), Krugman (1979,

1980), Melitz and Ottaviano (2005) and Melitz and Trefler (2012) have models based on imperfect competition and scale economies, with changing structure and composition of trade, exploration of the *dynamics of division of labor over space and time* and how they affect distant trading nations is necessary. Indeed, with ICT boons rapidly emerging, now especially it is imperative.

It is true that an economy that is insulated from competition but without access to global technology and global markets or a global supply chain can suffer from the benefits of "growth via interaction or communication" with developed nations (Helpman [2004], Lucas [1995]).[11] Although global trade slowed after 2010 following the financial crisis, it has rebounded. The present importance of trade and its growth impact can in no way be undermined, as is evidenced by a flurry of research (Eaton and Kortum [2012], Hanson [2012], Haskel et al. [2012], Helpman [2011], Melitz and Trefler [2012], World Bank [2020, 2021]).[12] However, the effects of trade on productivity growth are likely to be different across samples of countries (Dollar [1992], Frankel and Romer [1999], Goldberg et al. [2010a, 2010b], Iacovone, Rauch and Winters [2013]). Also, statistical evidence of a positive relationship between growth and trade does not have a well-crafted, consistent, theoretical framework accompanying it. As Lucas (2003, pp. 7–8) has opined: "[These] models support a compelling case for the importance of free trade. What they do not provide, though, is a theoretical link between free trade and economic growth that is both rapid and sustained." Typically, following Solow (2000), traditional growth theory based on exogenous technical progress has focused on trade and total factor productivity improvement. Subsequently, the emergence of endogenous growth theory has generated a voluminous literature emphasizing the role of "ideas," human capital and R&D, where technology via "creative destruction" plays a role (see Aghion and Howitt [2008], Helpman [2004], Romer [1990]). However, trade is necessary but not sufficient by itself to induce growth, except when skill and internal conditions are suitable (see Acemoglu [2009], Das [2002, 2015], Grossman and Helpman [1991a, 1991b], Lucas [2003], Stiglitz and Charlton [2007]).

With *TZ-based trade* (i.e., through virtual platforms), we find that ICT-led technological benefits bridging the agents located in separated TZs could induce growth via network effects. Often such exchange involves services or ideas (intangibles) that are eventually embedded in a physical product (final or intermediate tangibles). As we mentioned, gigantic leaps of technology,

---

[11] Helpman (2004, 2011) offers comprehensive readings on trade theories and economic growth in a nontechnical way.

[12] The *Journal of Economic Perspectives* held a four-paper symposium on new developments in trade theory in spring 2012. See www.aeaweb.org/issues/246#10.1257/jep.26.2.91.

declines in costs of communications and the growth of virtual commerce and the service sector taking advantage of TZ differences to combine tasks (division of labor) have led to such trade. So long as concern for *time-perishability* exists, intuitively taking advantage via ICT-led communication networks could be a vehicle for virtual transmission of source-to-client spillover benefits, thereby inducing the permanent growth of the recipient. In other words, VT has a "natural" mechanism for catalyzing the growth process along with trade in commodities by dint of extending the effective working hours, whereby product-ivity increases via global trade. It is "time-augmenting" technical change. As "round the clock" production is possible, twenty-four hours is the total time combined over, say, two TZs where stages of production are done in one suitable TZ (where people are naturally located and *time-based comparative advantage* exists) and the other TZ has no comparative advantage due to it being nighttime. Doubling the effective working hours to twenty-four, round the clock, causes productivity levels to rise, as well as real income. Here, VT causes growth without innovation explicitly taking place. This is similar to Lucas (2003, pp. 13–14) where "economic interactions on a daily basis" are *time-saving and trade-augmenting technical progress* with "dynamic scale economies" due to commu-nication networks but with an entirely different mechanism. Key differences are attributed to four interlinked factors, namely, (i) *communication network effects*: ICT-led reduction in delay, turning "physical distance" into opportunity; (ii) *trade-induced innovation and TOT effects*: joint increase in output and marginal productivity of capital with rise in capital stock; (iii) *efficient resource allocation effects* (effective use of TZ plus labor, capital) via intermediate inputs usage; and *(iv) investment rate effects*: augmented capital stock due to incentive for reinvest-ment of profit. Although Melitz and Trefler (2012) identify effects similar to (ii) and (iii), here it is entirely different due to TZ-led effects. *Without* skill con-straints, level and growth effects occur on a sustained basis (Kikuchi and Marjit [2011], Marjit and Mandal [2017]).

One must remember that trade theory is not really a theory of growth, although numerous empirical models do not seem to appreciate this idea. Trade is about reallocation of global resources that leads to a one-time rise in real income for countries participating in trade. It does not say anything about whether the rate of growth is affected by such reallocations. Gains from trade do not necessarily lead to growth. Ricardo was the first economist who developed a model of trade and endogenous growth (Findlay [1974]). It was through his framework that the import of cheaper corn translated into a decline in wage costs, which in turn induced an increase in the rate of profit, which then led to a higher growth rate for Great Britain that sustained the Industrial Revolution. Trade automatically led to growth, although all noticeable modern trade and endogenous growth models had to bring in technological change, innovations and R&D to explore such a relationship because trade as such never promises a higher growth rate. Interestingly, trade with differences in TZs replicates the original Ricardian result with a *different* mechanism.

As will be clear from Section 3, exogenous technical improvement in a developed North via ICT causes permanent growth in the South as the cost of production falls drastically with much quicker turnaround of output due to quick availability of intermediate business services sourced from the South. In this kind of simplistic setup, the marginal (and average) productivity of capital in the trade partners depends not only on the savings rate (exogenous) but also on the *delivery timeliness* couched in terms of the "iceberg cost effects" for TZ utilization. It also causes TOT improvement for less developed countries (LDCs, hereafter) which benefit from such virtual communication networks. This induces semi-endogenous *time-augmenting technical progress* in the destination. Within an *optimal growth framework* such as Ramsey-type intertemporal consumption, output *per time-unit* increases and hence growth occurs due to such time-augmenting changes via efficient utilization of intermediate input usages, and subsequently there is a further increase in profits investment.

Now in the context of the traditional formulation of trade–growth interlinkages, factor-biased technical change has distributional repercussions (wage-rental rate differentials) that are documented widely in growth and inequality literature. Debates surfaced in the late 1980s and early 1990s and continued thereafter about the role of (North–South) trade vis-à-vis skill-biased technological change (SBTC) in driving wage inequality, especially after the emergence of offshore outsourcing (see Bhagwati and Dehejia [1994], Chusseau, Dumont and Hellier [2008], Cravino and Sotelo [2019], Dreher and Gaston [2008], Jones and Marjit [2003], Kurokawa [2012] and Sachs and Shatz [1996]).[13] For a comprehensive overview, see Dorn, Clemens and Niklas (2021) and Helpman et al. (2012).

Recently, Wang, Findlay and Thangavelu (2021) ascribe a crucial role to trade indirectly affecting technology – via offshoring, firm heterogeneity, labor market frictions and global value chains – and, hence, wage inequality among workers. Cravino and Sotelo (2019) further show that *decline in trade costs* between 1995 and 2007 caused relocation of labor toward services with structural changes in trade, and, hence, that this accounts for wage premium as relative wages of unskilled workers fall as the goods sector shrinks.

With TZ effects, the main mechanism is due to the removal of the disutility of night-shift work. We also know that there exist wage differentials

---

[13] For general equilibrium models of trade and wage inequality, see Marjit (2008).

between day-shift and night-shift workers. This usually makes the wage payment higher in any country where night-shift is used. And such cost effect is much pronounced in the developed nations. This often induces them to shift part of the work to countries located in a different TZ, say in India or China where wage rates are usually low. However, VT tends to increase the wage gap as typically it is sector-biased technical progress that happens thanks to time-saving technological change in the business-services intermediates that go into the production of tangibles and other intangibles. Periodic intra-industry trade in labor services – due to "work-shift" features – causes labor allocation between day and night shifts, and scope for skill–unskilled inequality emerges. In fact, the mechanism is intuitive in that it shows how exploiting TZ differences can result in shifts of the relative supplies and demands for skilled workers globally, with corresponding impact on wage inequality. Due to connectedness via tasks sharing across service shifts, countries develop comparative advantage in the production of the shift-based sector. Exploiting such comparative cost advantage based on time-shifts means that trade expands.

1.4 Summary and Insights

We see that trade organized over virtual platforms is a new fourth dimension thanks to the ICT-enabled communication network reducing trade costs. Such "technology-induced" trade taking advantage of TZ differences is time-saving and trade-augmenting by nature; distance does not matter, unlike with traditional trade models. This is a clear point of departure from conventional trade theory. Such trade induces growth as timeliness of delivery matters. With the emergence of the new, fourth industrial revolution, virtual platforms could gain dominance and generate growth on a sustained basis with appropriate combinations of education, skill acquisition and capital. Using digital platforms to move the focus beyond manufacturing to services, digital infrastructure and adoption of technology are important for carving out new areas of comparative advantage. The ideas contained in this Element rest on the fundamental principle that if we really wish to capture virtual transactions, locally or globally, we must bring in the intrinsic virtue of "time" as a separate dimension of analysis. For international trade, beyond preference, endowment and technology, time is truly the fourth dimension that needs careful attention.

2 Theory and Pattern of Virtual Trade

2.1 Introduction

A central feature of the world economy is global interdependence as countries are intertwined through networks of trade, FDI and financial capital flows. With globalization in full swing – despite occasional hiccups – we need to comprehend what shapes the factors underlying trade, investment and the organization of production. A fundamental preoccupation in the theory of international trade is analyzing the basis of trade between nations and the factors driving patterns of trade. It is pertinent to mention here that Nobel laureate and legendary economic theorist Paul Samuelson, when asked by noted mathematician Stanislaw Ulam to name an "idea" in all of social sciences that is both true (important) and nonobvious, quite wittingly picked the principle of comparative advantage. It is known to all economists that the idea of comparative "cost" advantage has its origin in David Ricardo's all-time classic *Principles of Political Economy and Taxation* and has not lost its deep significance as a "tricky but brilliant theory" even today (Buccholz 2007). As outlined in Section 1, internalizing the role of ICT in facilitating VT is a paradigmatic shift that capitalizes on the "natural" comparative advantage of nonoverlapping locations. The role of "time" as a fourth catalyst and of country-specific communication networks in determining such comparative advantage is lacking in modern trade theory. In what follows, we show how the cornerstone of modern trade theory − based on three dimensions of preference, technology and endowments − could be extended to incorporate the additional fourth dimension of TZs.

It is established that three major contenders in the area of "basis of trade" are the Ricardian theory of comparative advantage, the HOS model of relative factor abundance and the increasing returns to scale (IRS) model pioneered by Paul Krugman. On these models, one may refer to Caves, Frankel and Jones (2007), Feenstra (2004), Feenstra and Taylor (2021), Helpman (2011) and Helpman and Krugman (1987). As mentioned in the introduction (Section 1), the utilization of TZ differences plays a crucial role for exchanges on virtual platform and needs due attention. In the Ricardian model, labor productivity differences play a crucial role in explaining trade patterns and specialization with one type of labor. In the specific-factor model of short-run variety, factor immobility, or factor specificity, is the crucial feature that leads to the emergence of trade and differences in factor returns. The long-run model where all factors are mobile is the most popular when it comes to explaining trade on the basis of relative factor endowments (at the macro level) and relative factor intensity in use (at the micro sectoral level). This is the HOS model. The role of time is not considered at all in any of these models or even in the "new" trade theory dealing with product diversification in an imperfect competition paradigm. As mentioned in Section 1, given the emergence of ICT-enabled network-based trade in services involving fragmented production stages, incorporating such elements into these workhorse models is the major focus of this section.

However, little work has appeared in terms of models that explicitly use the rate of time-preference as a determining factor. Notable among them is Sarkar (1985) who draws from earlier works of Ronald Findlay, later summarized in Findlay (1995) and Hicks (1973). It is a tradition in trade theory to look for primitives that explain patterns of trade. Such primitives evolve around the trinity – technology, endowment and taste. In this section, we propose another alternative that explains a significant part of trade in the contemporary world. We then use such idea for other standard trade models.

Let us take the case of a generalized HOS model as elaborated in Jones, Beladi and Marjit (1999). Countries are endowed with different amounts of various factors of production. They produce different bundles of similar or dissimilar goods. As the countries engage in trade, such goods are transported from one place to another. It is now well recognized that there are many kinds of trade, particularly in the service sector, that do not require physical shipment of goods. For example, programming problems are emailed from India to the USA at the end of the day (in India). American software specialists work on them in their regular office hours, while in India the office remains closed due to the time difference. When offices reopen in India, the solutions have already arrived, mainly as email attachments. This essentially means that business operations can continue almost for twenty-four hours a day, with very little interruption. This type of trade requires two basic preconditions. First, the difference in the TZs has to be such that the division of labor is feasible and the time difference can be properly utilized. Second, the technology should be such that the services can be transported quickly with little cost. The revolution in the IT sector has taken care of the second condition. Therefore, the first factor, namely, locations being in significantly separated TZs, becomes the primary driving force behind trade in the IT sector.

2.2 Time Zone Differences and Comparative Advantage in the Ricardian Model

Let us consider the Ricardian case and assume that two countries can produce X and Y with the following caveat. One unit of X is produced in two vertically related stages, each requiring one working day, whereas one unit of Y can be produced in one working day. There are two countries, the USA and India, which have the same technology for producing the goods, but they are located in different TZs. The Ricardian hypothesis says that they should not engage in trade with each other. So, in each of the two countries, production of one unit of X starts on Monday morning.[14] The first stage is finished by the end of Monday

---

[14] X should be a service that is intangible and does not require any physical shipment.

and the second stage starts on Tuesday morning. Therefore, one unit of X is ready for sale by Tuesday evening. For Y there is no such problem. It is ready for sale by Monday evening. But there is another pathway for trade. In this alternative way of doing trade, by Monday evening the first stage of X is finished and transported to the USA, which starts its Monday at that time and completes production by the time India wakes up on Tuesday morning.[15] Therefore, one unit of X is ready for sale as Tuesday starts. Such a trade method saves a day for X to be marketed. It is as if it requires half the time to market the same quantity of X. The time difference between India and the USA allows each of them to avail themselves of the product earlier than if they were to not trade with each other. With trade, the maximum available X in one day is doubled across the world with the level of Y remaining the same. This happens even if the physical productivity of the workers in both countries remains unchanged.

Now we present the basic idea in more detail. We have two economies and the ROW. We assume that the prices of X and Y, P_X and P_Y, are determined in the ROW. Given such prices, we need to determine the pattern of specialization. We also assume that Country A and some of the ROW are located in one TZ and Country B and the rest are located in the other. Countries A and B use the same Ricardian technology to produce X and Y and have the same labor endowments. One unit of labor is required to produce one unit X and β units are required to produce one unit of Y.[16] Markets are competitive. Production of Y is instantaneous in the sense that one unit of Y can be produced in one working day. But one unit of X requires production in two stages. Each stage requires one working day to complete. Half of the labor is used to produce the first stage and the other half the second. Committing one unit of labor to X implies that a unit of X is ready for sale after two working days whereas the alternative is to employ one unit of labor to produce Y and get one unit of Y after one working day. If P_X and P_Y are the commodity prices and W_A is the autarkic wage rate for Country A then:

$$W_A = \delta P_X \tag{1}$$

$$\beta W_A = P_Y \tag{2}$$

---

[15] Note that it does not matter which country produces the first stage and on which day. The main essence is the reduction in time for completion of the entire product.

[16] Here β is the unit labor requirement r Y. It is a fixed coefficient as in the Ricardian framework. However, in Section 2.2 we use α for the HOS model and this is a variable coefficient.

where $0 < \delta < 1$ is a rate of discount because X can be sold after two working days. This captures the idea that consumers like to have the product early. Countries A and B will produce only Y if:

$$\frac{1}{\delta\beta} > \frac{P_X}{P_Y}.$$ (3)

Also, assume that

$$\frac{1}{\delta\beta} > \frac{P_X}{P_Y} > \frac{1}{\beta},$$ (4)

that is, if somehow X could be delivered after one working day, as in the case of Y, neither of the countries would produce Y.

Since A and B are located in different TZs, workers in B can work while workers in A are resting, and vice versa. Markets open every twenty-four hours. The first half of the day can be used to produce the first stage of X in A; the partially completed X is then transferred it to B, which completes the second phase, and the product is ready for sale after one working day in A as well as in B.

Before trading together, A and B were identical and thus paid the same wages. Now, with vertical trade, the resultant wages are W_A^T, W_B^T. Then, for both of them to specialize in X, the following must hold:

$P_X - \frac{1}{2}\frac{P_Y}{\beta} > \frac{1}{2}\frac{P_Y}{\beta}$, that is,

$$\frac{P_X - \frac{1}{2}\frac{P_Y}{\beta}}{1/2} > \frac{P_Y}{\beta} \text{ for Country A and}$$ (5)

$$\frac{P_X - \frac{1}{2}\frac{P_Y}{\beta}}{1/2} > \frac{P_Y}{\beta} \text{ for Country B.}$$ (6)

Equation (5) suggests that for Country A, after paying the Country B workers the wage they were getting before, the new wage is higher than their opportunity cost, that is, the wage obtained from producing Y. Equation (6) implies the same for Country B.

Both Equations (5) and (6) hold if

$$\frac{P_X}{P_Y} > \frac{1}{\beta}.$$ (7)

Consider the competitive condition for X:

$$\frac{1}{2}W_A^T + \frac{1}{2}W_B^T = P_X > \frac{P_Y}{\beta}.$$ (8)

Since, initially, $W_A = W_B = \frac{P_X}{\beta}$, for Equation (8) to hold at least one country must get a higher wage now.

One should also note that we require a balancing condition such that the amount of goods-in-process released by A matches exactly the handling capacity of B. If L_A and L_B are given labor endowments, then

$$\frac{L_A}{1/2} = \frac{L_B}{1/2}.$$
(9)

Equation (9) must hold since by assumption $L_A = L_B$.

Traditional models of vertical trade in the Ricardian structure are provided by Marjit (1987) and Sanyal (1983) and in the HOS framework by Dixit and Grossman (1982). But these models assumed a pattern of intra-country comparative advantage across stages of production. The driving force behind trade here is the time difference. Even if both the countries have exactly the same technology for producing the various stages of X, they can still trade because they can take *advantage of the time difference*. The important thing is that Countries A and B should *not* produce both the stages on their own; rather, they each complete one stage.

Now we generalize the model and do away with redundant assumptions. We assume that $L_A \neq L_B$ and the stages of production of X are indexed in a continuum by $z \in [0, 1]$ with $m(z)$ denoting the requirement of labor to produce the zth stage for one unit of final X. This characterization is identical for both countries.

Furthermore, $\int_0^{\tilde{z}} m(z)dz = M(\tilde{z}).$
(10)

Here, $M(\tilde{z})$ is the cumulative function with the obvious property and reaching maximum at $M'(1) = 1$. Free trade equilibrium conditions then imply:

$$W_A^T M(\tilde{z}_1) + W_B^T \{1 - M(\tilde{z}_1)\} = P_X.$$
(11)

In what follows, $\dfrac{L_A}{M(\tilde{z}_1)} = \dfrac{L_B}{\{1 - M(\tilde{z}_1)\}} = X.$
(12)

Therefore, Country A will produce up to stage $\tilde{z}_1$th and the rest is produced by Country B. Hence, some observations are in order. First, $W_A^T = W_B^T = P_X$. If not, then shifting around the stages from one country to the other could reduce the average cost of producing X. Competition will rule that out. Second, $\tilde{z}_1$, derived from Equation (11), is one candidate for the equilibrium cut-off point. The other candidate will be $\tilde{z}_2$, implying:

$$\frac{L_A}{\{1 - M(\tilde{z}_2)\}} = \frac{L_B}{M(\tilde{z}_2)} \Rightarrow \frac{L_A}{L_B} = \frac{\{1 - M(\tilde{z}_2)\}}{M(\tilde{z}_2)}. \tag{13}$$

There is no guarantee that $\tilde{z}_1 = \tilde{z}_2$ except when $L_A = L_B$. The consistency requirement suggests that the cumulative labor intensities embodied in goods-in-process must be proportional to the relative labor endowments.

Third, the two countries are identical except that they are located in NOLTZs. We do not need to invoke the love for variety considerations in utility and increasing returns in production like Krugman (1979) to explain the reason behind trade. Interestingly, there is a similarity because the pattern of trade is indeterminate here, as in the Krugman model, but gains from trade nonetheless exist.

Two issues are noteworthy. First, transfer of technology in the international context has been quite an interesting dimension– see Singh and Marjit (2003). In particular, transfer of technology in the Ricardian trade model has been analyzed by Beladi, Jones and Marjit (1997) and Ruffin and Jones (2007). If initially Country B does not have the technology to produce X, Country A should costlessly transfer such technology to B so that B participates in the production of X. Since Country B does not have the technology to produce X, it will produce Y and earn $\frac{P_Y}{\beta}$. Again, when B cannot help A in producing X, A also specializes in Y and gets $\frac{P_Y}{\beta}$. By transferring technology to B, each can get $P_X > \frac{P_Y}{\beta}$.

Second, one can invoke iceberg-type shipment costs between A and B in our Ricardian model. This implies that one has to process $\frac{X}{s}$ units to process one unit of X. Assume $0 < s < 1$. This implies that $(1 - s)X$ will be lost in the process. Thus, the effective price is sP_X. Therefore, the new condition for a profitable X venture is

$$P_X > \frac{1}{s}\frac{P_Y}{\beta} \tag{14}$$

With $0 < s < 1$, Equation (14) is less likely to hold than without such transportation cost. We also know that initially $P_X > \frac{1}{\delta}\frac{P_Y}{\beta}$. Therefore, our arguments will go through if $s > \delta$, that is, if the benefit from exploiting the time difference exceeds that of the shipment cost. The benefits of technical changes on the trade pattern and specialization are undoubtedly significant in the case of VT.[17] With iceberg-type costs, the benefits of VT are reduced unless delivery timeliness

---

[17] For general equilibrium in the global economy, refer to Marjit, Mandal and Nakanishi (2020).

occurs by dint of exploiting ICT networks. Actually, exploiting NOLTZ differences is similar to the time-augmenting technical progress discussed earlier; utilizing such advantages gives a result that is akin to technological spillover across zones via ICT-enabled network benefits.

2.3 Time Zone Differences and Trade in the Heckscher–Ohlin–Samuelson Setup

Another workhorse of modern trade theory is the relative endowments-based explanation of specialization and trade given by the HOS model where countries have identical production technologies. Here, we invoke TZ issues in a basic 2×2 HOS model to elicit implications for TZ differences, given widespread ICT network boons.

Consider an economy producing two commodities X and Y. While X is essentially a service, Y is a tangible good. Let $S =$ supply of skilled labor; $K =$ supply of capital; $L =$ supply of unskilled labor; $X =$ service output; $Y =$ physical good; $a_{ij} =$ amount of ith factor used in production of one unit of jth commodity $(i = S, K$ and $j = X, Y); w_s =$ wage of skilled labor; $r =$ rent; $P_j =$ price of jth commodity; $\delta =$ discount factor; $\theta_{ij} =$ distributive share of ith factor in j^{th} commodity: $\lambda_{ij} =$ employment share of ith factor in j^{th} commodity.

Each good is produced using skilled labor (S) and capital (K) under constant returns to scale and sold in a perfectly competitive market. Prices are set in the world market and we assume small open economies (i.e., price-takers). Production of X requires two units of S and K.[18] We assume the technological coefficients to be fixed for the production of X while a_{sy} and a_{ky}, the technological coefficients of Y production, are considered to be variable. Following Marjit (2007) we assume the production of X to be divided into two stages.[19] Thus, the service is ready in two days and the consumer receives it on the third day. With such time taken for production and final delivery, the producer receives price $P_x\delta$, with P_x being the price of X and δ the discount factor. The

---

[18] Production of X is divided into two stages, each stage requiring one working day and each working day utilizing one unit of both labor and capital. Here, assumption of fixed coefficients in the services sector is alike to the Leontief variety and for analytical tractability, we adopt this following the Ricardian fixed unit factor requirement discussed in the previous section. However, that does not undermine our purpose because even with variable coefficient technology, the basic argument holds. The assumption is not crucial for our results. The only thing is that with relative price changes, a variable proportions assumption would trigger a mix of inputs usage without altering the factor intensity. This fixed proportion use of labor and capital in the service sector is realistic to some extent because service delivery usually involves constant proportion of labor-hours with a machine. Also, good Y could be assumed to be a numeraire with Py = 1. However, that does not affect the result. In other sections, we deal with that assumption; in this section, it is not explicitly mentioned as it would undermine our purpose.

[19] There is no night shift.

(exogenous) discount factor δ ($0 < \delta \leq 1$) captures the time-preference of the consumers. For further clarification, readers can see Marjit, Mandal and Nakanishi (2020) and check how δ is incorporated. The consumers want to get the product earlier and hence are willing to pay more for quicker delivery (i.e., there is a preference for timely consumption). So, if the service is delivered late, the value of δ falls; if it is delivered earlier, δ rises. Therefore, the cost–rice equation is given by[20]

$$w_s 2 + r2 = P_x \delta; \tag{15}$$

$$w_s a_{sy} + r a_{ky} = P_y \tag{16}$$

where w_s and r are wage and rent, respectively, and P_x and P_y denote the prices of good X and good Y, respectively. Also, we assume that (skilled) labor is used intensively in X whereas Y is a capital-intensive good. Factors are fully employed within both the sectors so that:

$$2X + a_{sy}Y = S; \tag{17}$$

$$2X + a_{ky}Y = K. \tag{18}$$

Solution of the model is quite well known in the trade literature (see Jones [1965]). We have four unknown variables – w_S, r, X and Y – to solve from Equations (15)–(18). Given the commodity prices, the factor prices are determined from Equations (15) and (18). Once the factor prices are solved, we have the values of technological coefficients through CRS (constant returns to scale) assumption. Once the $a_{ij}s$ are known, we can find outputs X and Y from Equations (17) and (18). So, the system is solvable. Of course, the relative endowments of S/K lie in the cone of diversification so that no factor-intensity reversals happen (see Jones [1965] and [2018] for elucidation).

2.3.1 Time Zone Utilization

One way to realize full value is for the producers of X to reduce the time required for production. This can be achieved when production is fragmented between two countries with nonoverlapping working hours. With this, the production process continues for twenty-four hours and consumers receive the product one day earlier. Following Mandal (2015), this pushes up the value of δ to 1. The producers thus obtain full value of the service. This change

---

[20] In this model, we do not split labor into skilled and unskilled categories and, hence, w = wage of unskilled labor is not used here in this model.

of δ from *less than 1* to 1 definitely benefits individual producers. It also affects factor prices and the level of output.[21]

To consider the effects on factor prices, we take the total differential of Equations (15) and (16) and express the percentage change with "∧" (see Jones [1965] for exposition) to derive:

$$\hat{w}_s \theta_{sx} + \hat{r} \theta_{kx} = \hat{\delta}\delta; \tag{19}$$

$$\hat{w}_s \theta_{sy} + \hat{r} \theta_{ky} = 0. \tag{20}$$

With a relatively higher price (because of a rise in δ), production of X becomes more lucrative, and that further boosts demand for factors used in X, resulting in changes in factor prices. Eventually, the wage rises and the rental rate falls.[22] This follows from the Stolper–Samuelson effect as X is relatively skill-intensive while Y uses capital more intensively.

Using Equations (19) and (20) we get these changes in the wage and rental rate:

$$\hat{w}_s = \hat{\delta}\delta \left(\frac{\theta_{ky}}{|\theta|} \right) > 0; \tag{21}$$

$$\hat{r} = (-) \left(\frac{\theta_{sy}}{|\theta|} \right) \hat{\delta}\delta < 0 \tag{22}$$

where, $|\theta| = \theta_{sx}\theta_{ky} - \theta_{sy}\theta_{kx};$ \tag{23}

$|\theta| = \theta_{sx}\theta_{ky} - \theta_{sy}\theta_{kx} > 0;$ since $\theta_{sx} > \theta_{sy}$ and $\theta_{kx} < \theta_{ky}$. It is apparent from the above equations that the direction of change depends on the factor intensity of X and Y, as well as on the change in the discount rate.

2.3.2 Output Effects

As Y production is characterized by variable coefficient technology, the amount of labor and capital involved in its production can be altered, and the relatively dearer skilled labor can be substituted by cheaper capital. To identify such variation, we use the elasticity of substitution between two factors as:

$$\sigma_y = \frac{\hat{a}_{sy} - \hat{a}_{ky}}{\hat{r} - \hat{w}_s} \Rightarrow \hat{a}_{sy} = \hat{a}_{ky} + (\hat{r} - \hat{w}_s)\sigma_y. \tag{24}$$

---

[21] It is to be noted that δ is exogenous and enters the cost–price equation via its effect on consumers' evaluation of faster or delayed delivery. Hence, it might be construed as a time-saving technical change parameter with factor-neutral effects. This has a bearing on NOLTZ utilization, prompting faster delivery via productivity (and, hence, cost) benefits.

[22] This follows from Stolper–Samuelson results.

Using the envelope condition:

$$\hat{a_{sy}}\theta_{sy} + \hat{a_{ky}}\theta_{ky} = 0 \Rightarrow \hat{a_{sy}} = (-)\frac{\theta_{ky}}{\theta_{sy}}\hat{a_{ky}} => \hat{a_{ky}} = (-)\frac{\theta_{sy}}{\theta_{ky}}\hat{a_{sy}}.$$

Substituting this in Equation (23) and using Equation (22) we get:

$$\hat{a_{sy}} = (-)\delta\hat{\delta}\frac{\theta_{ky}}{|\theta|}\sigma_y; \qquad (25)$$

$$\hat{a_{ky}} = \delta\hat{\delta}\frac{\theta_{sy}}{|\theta|}\sigma_y. \qquad (26)$$

Costly factors will be substituted by relatively cheaper ones where the rate of factor substitution is given by the elasticity of substitution between S and K. This is shown as follows:

$$\sigma_y = \frac{\hat{a_{sy}} - \hat{a_{ky}}}{\hat{r} - \hat{w_s}} \Rightarrow \hat{a_{sy}} = \hat{a_{ky}} + (\hat{r} - \hat{w_s})\sigma_y => \hat{a_{ky}} = \hat{a_{sy}} - (\hat{r} - \hat{w_s})\sigma_y.$$

The above equations show the change in factor employment in production of one unit of Y when the other sector (X) utilizes the TZ difference between two countries for production. This phenomenon is diagrammatically represented in Figure 4.

In Figure 4, Equation (17) has been plotted as the S constraint while Equation (18) is plotted as the K constraint. The initial equilibrium is at E_1 where the economy produces X_1 and Y_1. When the effective price of X rises because of an increase in δ, production of X becomes more lucrative. As explained earlier, *factor-intensity assumptions* cause excess demand for S and excess supply of K. Thus, the wage rises and the rent falls. Since factor requirements depend on factor prices, $\hat{a_{SY}} < 0$, $\hat{a_{KY}} > 0$. Thus, as we see in Figure 4, changes in a_{SY} and a_{KY} cause the labor and capital constraints to move along the Y axis. The S constraint moves outward and the new equilibrium is at E_2. This shows a higher output of X (at X_2) and a lower Y (at Y_2). For the changes in the equilibrium level of X and Y we take the total differential of Equations (17) and (18).

Therefore,

$$\hat{X}\lambda_{SX} + \hat{Y}\lambda_{SY} + \lambda_{SY}\hat{a_{sy}} = 0;$$

$$\hat{X}\lambda_{KX} + \hat{Y}\lambda_{KY} + \lambda_{KY}\hat{a_{ky}} = 0.$$

Substituting the values of $\hat{a_{sy}}$ and $\hat{a_{ky}}$ and applying the Cramer's rule[23] gives:

---

[23] $|\lambda| = \begin{vmatrix} \lambda_{SX} & \lambda_{SY} \\ \lambda_{KX} & \lambda_{KY} \end{vmatrix}$ and $\left[\lambda_{SX} = \frac{a_{SX}X}{S}; \lambda_{SY} = \frac{Ya_{SY}}{S}; \lambda_{KX} = \frac{a_{KX}X}{K}; \lambda_{KY} = \frac{Ya_{KY}}{K}\right].$

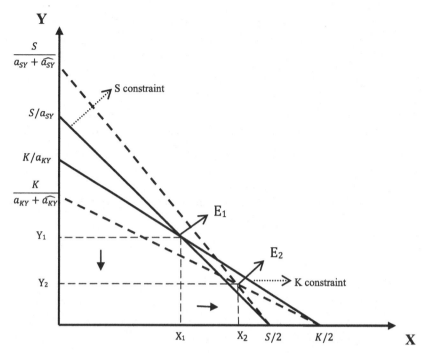

Figure 4 Changes in output with alterations in factor requirement

$$\hat{X} = \frac{1}{|\lambda|}\frac{1}{|\theta|}\left(\theta_{ky}\lambda_{SY}\lambda_{KY} + \theta_{sy}\lambda_{KY}\lambda_{SY}\right)\sigma_y\delta\hat{\delta}. \tag{27}$$

This implies that there would be an increase in output of X (Figure 4) due to utilization of TZ difference. Correspondingly, output of Y falls.

$$\hat{Y} = (-)\frac{1}{|\lambda|}\frac{1}{|\theta|}\left(\theta_{sy}\lambda_{SX}\lambda_{KY} + \theta_{ky}\lambda_{KX}\lambda_{SY}\right)\sigma_y\delta\hat{\delta} < 0 \tag{28}$$

Here, the direction of change is independent of the factor intensity as both $|\lambda|$ and $|\theta|$ have the same signs. Both of these having the same signs follows from the assumption that relatively skilled abundant nations allocate more workers to the X sector, and X and Y are relatively skilled and capital-intensive, respectively. Even with unaltered factor intensity, TZ utilization drives the key result. Thus, utilizing TZ difference has a major effect on the output of different sectors where the sector exploiting the TZ difference expands and the other contracts. When $\delta = \delta$ (D) is incorporated in the model, contrary to the gravity model we see that distance does not deter trade; rather, it benefits the X sector to have more trade as distance rises in NOLTZs. Also, it leads to a positive change in wage rate with intensive use of labor in X relative to Y. This signifies that as the trading partners are geographically far apart, utilizing communication networks facilitates virtual transactions occurring across the NOLTZs. This is unlike the conventional gravity model without considering the scope of VT enhanced by IT-enabled benefits. Hence, as mentioned in Section 1, ICT-enabled networks facilitate trade via faster completion of various production stages, leading to quicker production and consumption, which surely reflect gains. Thus, like a technological progress equivalent to reduction in time required for production and consumption, trade across NOLTZs also implies time-augmenting technical change.

2.4 Time Zone Differences and a Monopolistically Competitive Model

Here we construct a simple monopolistically competitive model of trade drawing on Dixit and Stiglitz (1977), Krugman (1979) and Marjit (2007) and where TZ differences can easily be brought in. However, the setup we propose here heavily depends on Kikuchi (2011). Let there be three goods – X, Y and Z – and three countries – A, B and D – that are strategically located in NOLTZs. Nonoverlapping working hours are eight hours in A, B and D, ordered in a sequence. In such circumstances, the entire twenty-four hours of any calendar date could be used for production purposes.

Apart from TZ differences, these countries are identical. They have the same technologies of production and the same endowments of labor, L. Both X and Y are consumption goods and tradable, while Z is a business service that is used as an intermediate input to produce X. Hence, Z is not necessarily internationally traded, per se, and is supplied by monopolistically competitive firms. Note that Z has n number of varieties that require two consecutive stages of production. A part of each variety of Z may be outsourced to another country. Markets for X and Y are perfectly competitive, and both of them are produced under CRS. Further, Y uses L, and one L produces one unit of Y. The wage rate is normalized to unity. Moreover, X is produced by differentiated Z such that the production function is:

$$X = \left(\sum_{i=1}^{n} z_i^{\rho}\right)^{1/\rho}; \ 0 < \rho < 1. \tag{29}$$

The cost function is:

$$C = \left(\sum_{i=1}^{n} P_i^{\rho/(\rho-1)}\right)^{(\rho-1)/\rho}. \tag{30}$$

Here n is the number of differentiated intermediate inputs, z_i stands for quantity of ith variety and P_i is the price of ith variety of Z. The elasticity of substitution between two varieties is $\sigma = 1/_{(1-\rho)}$ where $\sigma > 1$ as $0 < \rho < 1$. It is a constant elasticity of substitution case.

Production of Z requires both fixed cost and variable cost. Fixed cost is denoted by α units of labor, and variable cost requires two units of labor for one unit of output. Two consecutive stages are finished with two L, each stage requiring one unit of L. But these two stages are not necessarily produced in one country. If they are produced in more than one country, ICT is needed. So, we may have two different cost structures. When Z is produced in one country (no trade in intermediate inputs), the unit cost function becomes:

$$TC_i = w(\alpha + 2z_i); \quad i = 1, 2, 3, \ldots, n. \tag{31}$$

Thus, following the standard Dixit–Stiglitz (1977) framework:

$$P = 2^{\sigma w}/_{(\sigma - 1)}. \tag{32}$$

Hence, the long-run zero-profit condition yields:

$$z = \frac{\alpha}{2}(\sigma - 1). \tag{33}$$

Following Marjit (2007) we postulate that outsourcing the second stage of production may lead to early delivery of the intermediate input. In terms of cost, the labor requirement falls from 2 to $(1 + \beta) < 2$ as $0 < \beta < 1$. This also requires certain cost in the form of ICT. Let it be γ that is a kind of fixed cost. So, the cost function with ICT can be represented by:

$$TC_i^T = w(\alpha + \gamma + (1 + \beta)z_i). \tag{34}$$

The equilibrium price becomes:

$$P^T = \{(2 - 1 + \beta)\sigma w\}/_{(\sigma - 1)} = \{(1 + \beta)\sigma w\}/_{(\sigma - 1)}$$

$$\Rightarrow P^T = \{(2 - \xi)\sigma w\}/_{(\sigma - 1)}; \quad \text{where} = \xi(1 - \beta). \tag{35}$$

In what follows, the long-run zero-profit condition is:

$$z^T = \left[(\alpha + \gamma)/_{(2 - \xi)}\right](\sigma - 1). \tag{36}$$

Using Equations (31)–(33) in Equation (30) we get:

$$C = n^{1/(1-\sigma)}P = \left[P(z)^{1/\sigma}\right]X^{-1/\sigma}. \tag{37}$$

Again, from Equations (34)–(36) we deduce:

$$C^T = n^{1/(1-\sigma)}P = \left[P^T\left(z^T\right)^{1/\sigma}\right]X^{-1/\sigma}. \tag{38}$$

A careful investigation of Equations (37) and (38) reveals that there are two competing effects influencing C^T; γ raises it while ξ leads to a reduction of C^T. In other words, whether outsourcing is helpful depends on whether the cost of ICT is less than the benefit rendered by early delivery of the intermediate inputs. This can be expressed as follows:

$$\frac{C^T}{C} = \left(\frac{2-\xi}{2}\right)^{(\sigma-1)/\sigma}\left(\frac{\alpha+\gamma}{\alpha}\right)^{1/\sigma}. \tag{39}$$

Equation (39) may be rewritten as:

$$\left(\frac{C^T}{C}\right)^{\sigma/(\sigma-1)} = \left(\frac{2-\xi}{2}\right)\left(\frac{\alpha+\gamma}{\alpha}\right)^{1/(\sigma-1)}. \tag{40}$$

Hence, we argue that if $\left(\frac{C^T}{C}\right)^{\sigma/(\sigma-1)} < 1$, outsourcing of unfinished intermediate input to a country located in a NOLTZ is beneficial.

Now we need to check what happens to the goods market if all three countries, A, B and D, are open for international trade. Turning to the autarkic case, the autarkic price of X would be:

$$P_X = \left[P(z)^{1/\sigma}\right]X^{-1/\sigma}. \tag{41}$$

To close the model, we assume a Cobb–Douglas preference for a representative individual as:

$$U = X^\mu Y^{(1-\mu)}. \tag{42}$$

So, pretrade the numbers of varieties (and firms), P_X and X, are:

$$n = \mu L/\alpha\sigma; \tag{43}$$

$$P_X = (\mu L/\alpha\sigma)^{1/(1-\sigma)}\left[\,2\sigma/(\sigma-1)\right]; \tag{44}$$

$$X = (\mu L/\alpha)^{\sigma/(\sigma-1)}(\alpha)^{1/(1-\sigma)}[(\sigma-1)/2]. \tag{45}$$

Also, we assume that all countries produce Y to start with. Consider that countries A and B are connected through ICT whereas D is not. So, A and B can virtually trade in business services. In that case: $\left(\frac{C^T}{C}\right)^{\sigma/(\sigma-1)} < 1$.

Note that country D has nothing to do with the outsourcing business between A and B. In spite of that, VT between A and B yields gain. The reasons are: (1) the numbers of available business services and firms increase; and (2) the price of business services, P, is reduced, resulting in a reduction in P_X. Therefore, connected countries would specialize in the production of both X and Z following comparative advantage. The size of the market for X is also enhanced as P_X goes down; on the other hand, Country D's service sector dwindles. Thus, again, the increase in exports leads to further specialization and cost reduction. Hence, we argue that, in a connected world, exploitation of TZ differences through cheaper cost of ICT leads to specialization in business service.

Now, consider the welfare implication of such trade. Post-trade, the number of firms is:

$$n^T = 3\mu L/_{(\alpha+\gamma)}\sigma. \tag{46}$$

The equilibrium price of X in the post-trade situation is:

$$P_X^T = [3\mu L/_{(\alpha+\gamma)}\sigma]^{1/(1-\sigma)}[(2-\xi)\sigma/_{(\sigma-1)}]. \tag{47}$$

The equilibrium quantity of X is:

$$X^T = (3\mu L/_\sigma)^{\sigma/(\sigma-1)}(\alpha+\gamma)^{1/(1-\sigma)}[(\sigma-1)/_{(2-\xi)}]. \tag{48}$$

However, whether P_X^T is less than P_X is not apparent. This depends on:

$$[3\alpha/_{(\alpha+\gamma)}]^{1/(1-\sigma)}[(2-\xi)/_2] = \left[\frac{(2-\xi)}{2}\right]\left[\frac{(\alpha+\gamma)}{\alpha}\right]^{1/(\sigma-1)}\left[\frac{1}{3}\right]^{1/(\sigma-1)}. \tag{49}$$

Therefore, if $\left(\frac{C^T}{C}\right)^{\sigma/(\sigma-1)} < 1$, and the above condition holds true, all the countries, A, B and D, would gain, irrespective of whether all are connected through ICT and located in overlapping or nonoverlapping TZs. If any two of these three countries take part in VT, all can gain from such trade.

In the preceding sections, we introduced the elements of a fourth dimension, namely, TZ differences based on the natural comparative advantage of location in three cornerstones of modern trade theory. In all three cases, virtual connectivity between countries located in NOLTZs yields substantial benefits and counters the adverse effect of distance via ICT-led communication networks. Appropriating such benefits, unlike with conventional gravity models, reduces trade costs and the iceberg effects of distance via timely delivery and increases accrual of gains to both consumers and producers. Section 2.5 delves deep into the mechanism.

2.5 Distance, Production and Virtual Trade

As mentioned in Section 1, most standard analysis in international trade has missed the elements of the pervasive fragmentation of the production process and, hence, modeling international organization of production across locations in distinct TZs. In practice, slicing of the global value chain depends on integration of TZs to bridge the distances.

Typically, physical distance between trading nations hinders trade. In this context, trade restriction, transportation and trading costs are the prime factors deterring global trade. The Ricardian model with trading cost, the HOS model with transportation, the intra-industry trade model with traders and the gravity model of trade corroborate such a claim. Anderson (2000), Anderson and van Wincoop (2004), Bahar (2020), Bernard, Jensen and Schott (2006), Cassing (1978), Chakrabarti (2004), Davis (1998), Deardorff (2004), Falvey (1976), Feenstra (2004) and Limao and Venables (2001) are some of the noted contributions in this line of research. In a recent study, Baldwin and Dingel (2021) have discussed the possibility of COVID-19-led remote work going overseas, namely, telemigration and offshorability of teleworkable jobs as more service trade picks up, and find from gravity model estimates that large asymmetric increase in service tasks from low-wage nations can occur even with a small rise in trade costs.

In recent times, however, the composition of trade has changed to a certain extent with the emergence of offshoring of business services such as engineering, consulting and software development. Sleuwaegen and Smith (2021) have shown that "service characteristics" have four dimensions, namely, intangibility, inseparability (between buyer and seller), time-perishability (nonstorable) and variability (less general) in a continuum of characteristics. The striking feature of such trade is the nonnecessity of physical shipment of products. Coupled with this possibility, we are also confronted with the issue of separated or nonoverlapping TZs (explained already). Further, with the advent of high-bandwidth Internet, trade in virtual services, which is virtual in nature, has become relatively less costly. Baldwin and Dingel (2021) mention the radical decline in trade costs for moving stuff, especially weightless things (ideas, data or services) compared to heavy stuff (goods); this decline in trade costs also affects the prospects of jobs going "offshore" in convenient time-locations. We already know that difference in TZs is often a matter only of physical distance (in terms of latitude). Thus, whether distance is a hindering factor for trade has become a questionable issue again. To date, only a handful of work has been done in the interface of trade and distance-related TZs. This includes Anderson (2014), Head, Mayer and Ries (2009), Kikuchi (2011), Mandal (2015), Marjit, Mandal and Nakanishi (2020) and Matsuoka and Fukushima (2010). Most of these papers look at the effect of NOLTZs on patterns of trade, volumes of trade, and welfare implications in a market setup that is monopolistic in nature.

It is apparent that the total volume of trade has two components: physical trade and trade in services including VT. Physical trade falls with distance. However, we are focusing on the relationship between VT and distance. The idea of VT is essentially trade in services or labor tasks that can be exported and imported back via the Internet. This part is relatively less explored in the existing literature. In this Element, we are ths attempting to relate the physical distance influencing (non)overlapping TZs between two trading partners with VT. Notice that this kind of trade has become a central issue only since the information technology revolution. The world being circular, TZs are essentially the reflection of aerial distance. Therefore, the distance between two places is exhibited by the difference in TZs. Hence, in the hindsight of the literature on TZ-driven trade, there is physical distance that triggers VT positively. Based on this wisdom, we now explore how distance can affect trade volume.

Drawing from Kikuchi and Marjit (2011), we consider a Cobb–Douglas production function for service output (S) that requires capital (K) and an intermediate input (m). The production function is given as:

$$S = K^{\alpha}(m)^{\frac{1-\alpha}{2}}(m)^{\frac{1-\alpha}{2}} = K^{\alpha}m^{1-\alpha}. \tag{50}$$

Note that $0 < \alpha < 1$.

For simplicity, we assume that one unit of L is required to produce one unit of m, which is assumed as the numeraire. Production of S requires two consecutive stages or workdays, and hence two m. But as in-home production needs two workdays, goods cannot be delivered in a timely manner. Untimely delivery of final goods/services is not desired by consumers. This would be reflected in the effective price of the final good or service, P_S. The extent of delay in delivery is negatively related to the consumers' valuation of the good.

Unlike before, let us denote the trade-related cost (i.e., any kind of transaction cost plus transport cost including opportunity cost of delay) by $\chi(D)$ where $\chi'(D) > 0$ so that, following a conventional explanation, as D rises, $\chi(D)$ increases. Let D have three ranges of distance values such that $D \in [D_{min},$

D_{mid}, D_{max}] for minimum, average and maximum distance specific to location. Further, D_{min} means an almost overlapping TZ with low χ. As D rises to, say, D_{mid}, gradually a *partial* NOLTZ comes in and $\chi(D)$ rises. *With VT,* $\chi(D)$ shrinks by exploiting the TZs via ICT networks. The polar case of D_{max} means *perfectly* NOLTZs with no VT taking place, and $\chi(D)$ further rises, approaching unity. Hence, we can write

$\chi'(D) > 0 \,\forall\, D_{min} < D < D_{max}$, with $VT\chi'(D) < 0 \,\forall\, D_{mid} < D < D_{max}$, and $\chi'(D) > 0 \,\forall\,$ $D > D_{max}$ with no VT. As $\chi(D)$ rises, the effective price received by the producer falls as consumers' valuation is negatively related to increase in χ.

The cost function for S is:

$$C = m + m. \tag{51}$$

For brevity, we assume that capital is costless. Therefore, the consumers' price (effective price of the product or service) would be $\frac{P_S}{\chi}$.

The demand for intermediate service input is determined by the standard profit maximization problem for S. The profit equation (assuming $P_S = 1$) is

$$\pi = \frac{P_S}{\chi} S - (m + m).$$

The first-order condition for profit maximization leads to

$$m = K\left(\frac{P_S}{2}\right)^{\frac{1}{\alpha}} (1 - \alpha)^{\frac{1}{\alpha}} \tag{52}$$

where $0 < \alpha < 1$. Hence,

$$S = K(P_S)^{\frac{1-\alpha}{\alpha}} \left(\frac{1 - \alpha}{2}\right)^{\frac{1-\alpha}{\alpha}} (\chi)^{\frac{\alpha-1}{\alpha}}. \tag{53}$$

It is apparent from Equation (53) that χ has a negative connotation for the volume of S. This is the cost of untimely delivery for not utilizing TZ difference. If countries exploit the opportunity of NOLTZs with others, they could get any one of the two stages of input processing done in a nonoverlapping country's workday. Hence, NOLTZs induce utilization of even nighttime for the purpose of production, making producers capable of delivering the final output in good time. Therefore, against this backdrop, the cost equation remains the same but the profit with exploitation of TZ differences changes to[24]

---

[24] Subscript "t" indicates exploiting the benefit rendered by TZ difference and IC networks.

$$\pi_t = P_S S - (m + m).\tag{54}$$

Therefore, the profit-maximized production equation is:

$$S_t = K(P_S)^{\frac{1-a}{a}}\left(\frac{1-\alpha}{2}\right)^{\frac{1-a}{a}}.\tag{55}$$

Comparing Equations (54) and (55) it is evident that for given K and L the quantity of S would be higher if TZ benefit is exploited.

$$S_t = K(P_S)^{\frac{1-a}{a}}\left(\frac{1-\alpha}{2}\right)^{\frac{1-a}{a}} > S = K(P_S)^{\frac{1-a}{a}}\left(\frac{1-\alpha}{2}\right)^{\frac{1-a}{a}}(\chi)^{\frac{a-1}{a}} \ (\text{as } 0 < \alpha < 1)$$

We mentioned earlier that difference in TZs depends on physical distance, D, that is:

$$\chi = \chi(D)\tag{56}$$

where $\chi'(D) > 0$ when countries are located in NOLTZs (maximum aerial distance).[25] We further consider that the distance between two places can be covered along the diameter of the globe (circle).[26]

Following this thought process, we see that not only does the service production increase but, along with it, a double (at most) amount of m compared to S is traded. A part of S (after the first stage) is exported first and then it is imported back after the final stage is done. A similar kind of trade pattern can be experienced for both the trading partners, as countries are free to allocate resources between intermediate input and final production. For both the countries, the final output is, in fact, timely delivered on an identical calendar date, although there would be difference in the time of delivery due to the TZ difference. This implies a surge or abrupt increase in trade volume, only because of VT.

Now we plug $\chi = \chi(D)$ into the profit-maximizing level of output. Therefore,

---

[25] The argument is built on the assumption that the globe is circular and distances between places are measured aerially.

[26] If we consider linear distance or traveling through the circumference of the circle, the relationship between *distance and trade* will exhibit an inverted U-shape. Volume of virtual trade will increase with distance, first indicating an increase in nonoverlapping stretch (day or night). Further, $\chi(D)$ and D are related via an S-shaped curve.

$$S_t = K(P_S)^{\frac{1-\alpha}{\alpha}} \left(\frac{1-\alpha}{2}\right)^{\frac{1-\alpha}{\alpha}} (\chi(D))^{\frac{\alpha-1}{\alpha}}. \tag{57}$$

Thus, as distance rises, χ gradually rises due to trade costs. So, *without VT*, S falls with rise in χ. However, *with VT*, S rises with rise in χ. S reaches the maximum when D_{max} corresponds exactly to the NOLTZs associated with maximum distance along the diameter of the globe.

For a small country framework, without changing the TOT, the volume of trade rises. This implies an unambiguous increase in welfare. Even if the countries are large, and if trade in final goods/services is not allowed, an increase in the volume of trade due to trade in the intermediate input will increase welfare. Now, assume a constant savings rate (ρ) so that we have the following capital equation:

$$\dot{K} = \rho S_t - \varphi K \tag{58}$$

where φ is the rate of depreciation of capital K. Therefore, $\dot{K}$ is the growth rate of capital. Thus,

$$\frac{\dot{K}}{K} = \rho(P_S)^{\frac{1-\alpha}{\alpha}} \left(\frac{1-\alpha}{2}\right)^{\frac{1-\alpha}{\alpha}} (\chi(D))^{\frac{\alpha-1}{\alpha}} - \varphi. \tag{59}$$

It is evident that as distance (D) increases and the value of χ goes down (*due to VT and TZ exploitation*), the increase in capital accumulation eventually leads to continuous output growth. We discuss this in detail in Section 3. The verbal upshot of the imperfectly competitive model is that there are substantial welfare benefits due to: (i) organization of trade in unfinished intermediate services thanks to virtual division of labor across multiple TZs; (ii) quicker production and delivery exploiting the comparative advantage of participating countries and generating consumption gains with preference for early delivery of final goods and services; (iii) all these translating into lower prices of final goods utilizing outsourced intermediate inputs; (iv) numbers of firms and corresponding outputs increasing due to connectivity; (v) via enhanced trade in intermediates, TZ exploitation enabling capital accumulation and inducing growth in the long run, equivalent to intermediate-input augmenting technical change; and, (vi) unlike the perfectly competitive models discussed in Sections 2.1 and 2.2, trade costs and iceberg effects of distance having a more predominant effect via trade in intermediates.

2.6 Summary and Insights

In this section, we extended the traditional workhorse trade models to incorporate the features of (i) utilization of TZ differences across nonoverlapping countries and (ii) ICT-enabled communication networks. We also discussed the beneficial role of TZ difference in successfully achieving consumers' time-preference for production and consumption, and in reducing trade costs and iceberg effects due to flourishing communication technology. In all these TZ-augmented trade models, time-saving technical change plays a central role. Why? This is simply because exploiting natural comparative advantage based on location leads to specialization in stages (fragments) of production via taking advantage of day–night cycles of twenty-four hours across two (or more) trade partners. In the case of the HOS setup, factor intensity and changes in the discount rate for time matter for factor–price effects and the sector, fragmenting production in suitable TZ gains from trade as output expands at the cost of the others who don't make use of the time gap. With a rise in distance, there is much more scope for utilizing TZ gaps, which could also increase the wage of the workers in the sector that is offshoring and using workers relatively intensively. In the monopolistic competition model, the result is that trade in intermediate business services leads to a lower price of the final good, and hence causes a rise in the equilibrium output of virtually connected firms through intermediation and increases the number of firms. Unlike the canonical gravity model, here the novelty is that distance does not deter trade; rather, with capital accumulation, output grows, causing trade to expand. This has implications for deep trade agreements like free trade agreements where conventional explanation harps on typical forces based on the gravity model and its applications.

3 Trade, Growth and Factor Income

3.1 Introduction

During the last few decades, the offshoring of business services such as engineering, consulting and software development has flourished to a considerable degree without the requirement of physical shipment of products.[27] The availability of global high-bandwidth network infrastructure has made it possible to organize production offshore. In other words, due to ICT breakthroughs and enabled services, the decline in trade and transaction costs has accelerated such trade in business services. Furthermore, taking advantage

---

[27] For brevity, we will refer to both ICT services and business process outsourcing (BPO) as "business services."

of such networked communications due to digitization of NOLTZ differences across geographically separated countries may become a primary driving force behind business-services trade. In fact, this has happened already; India's case is a good starting point, among others (World Bank [2020, 2021]).

Given the trade-augmenting and time-saving nature of such trade, we can envisage a growth mechanism. Unlike the typical trade models – which emphasize resource reallocation and allocative efficiency with rises in real income – VT could generate growth and level effects by improving productivity and boosting investment rate. We can see that ICT-enabled utilization of the advantages of TZ difference could bring time-saving technological improvements, leading to a permanent increase in productivity.

In the existing literature on growth and trade, however, relatively few attempts have been made to address the effect of TZs on growth. The main purpose of this section is to illustrate, with simple growth theory, how a time-saving improvement in business-services trade benefiting from TZ differences can have an impact on productivity and/or growth.[28] In fact, when value chains are fragmented over different geographical distances (longitudinal), such utilization of the benefits of NOLTZ differences through communication networks enabling imported intermediate business-services trade could accelerate the completion of a final project and make possible quick delivery with low shipping costs. This is a kind of "trade-augmenting" technical change. As virtual network-based communication has become a tour de force for trade, this, no doubt, has opened new vistas of research on trade-induced growth. The next section reviews and discusses such a mechanism and how it contributes to sustained growth.

3.2 Review of Existing Literature and the Connection with Virtual Trade

Whether global integration is beneficial for economic growth and how it affects returns to factors in an open world trading system via harmonization of institutions (e.g., under GATT or WTO-based trade laws and regulations) are some intriguing problems economists have been facing for a long time (see Frankel [1997], Irwin [1996], Sachs and Warner [1995], Stiglitz and Charlton [2007]

---

[28] At the very outset of this section we want to make one confession, namely, that in a single section it is impossible to even touch upon the concerns hovering around the trade and growth interface. So, we picked up two strands – dynamic and static. We then tried to harp on a few contemporary growth and income distribution dimensions that go well with trade. We understand that the scheme may sound a bit ad hoc, but this is what we could do within the ambit of the purpose of the Element. We have done this with the intention that this Element may form the building block for further research on TZ-induced trade, growth and distribution in both static and dynamic models.

and Williamson [1998]). In this section, being parsimonious, we scratch the surface by touching upon the existing studies then focusing on the relatively neglected issue of VT based on the ICT-networks-induced communication revolution that is bringing about global interconnectedness.

As mentioned in Section 1, trade openness, development and growth comprise a familiar area of research. For a comprehensive overview of the issues, see Acharyya and Marjit (2014), Aghion and Durlauf (2005), Aghion and Howitt (2008), Alesina, Spolaore and Wacziarg (2005), Bardhan (2003), Findlay (1984) and Ventura (2005). For a range of research (theoretical as well as some empirical) on issues such as international labor migration, FDI and multinational firms, globalization and institutional differences, trade and poverty, trade and income distribution, fragmentation or outsourcing, and technology transfer, see Acharyya and Kar (2013), Grossman and Rogoff (2005), Marjit (2008) and Rodrik (2007). Some of the most well-known empirical research providing statistical evidence on trade's positive effect on income and growth is contained, for example, in Dollar (1992), Frankel and Romer (1999), Sachs and Warner (1995) and Sala-i-Martin (1997). However, Rodriguez and Rodrik (2001) and Rodrik, Subramanian and Rebbi (2002) find that institutional and structural factors are more important than trade policy. All these studies show that trade has a positive effect on growth via resource allocation effects according to comparative advantage, specialization, domestic and international competition with trade regimes, and international flows of capital and goods, as well as technology. The growth episodes of South Korea, Japan and China and other East Asian miracle stories along with other developing open economies can be adduced to support the fact that both judicious trade-led market expansion and internal factors matter in a complementary way (Helpman [2004], Lucas [1995]).

The different factors that paved the way for the rise in global trade are reduced trade costs, reduced transaction costs, and technological revolution, especially now, since the third industrial revolution was aided by general-purpose technologies, namely, ICT, as well as the recent developent of AI (see Brynjolfsson and McAfee [2014], Hidalgo [2015], Sridhar [2019]). However, such technological breakthroughs are important for trade as transmission of knowledge and high-technology-intensive products are vehicled through trade and investment. For example, the WTO's ITA has brought about several trade facilitation measures promoting e-commerce and e-business, as well as ICT-enabled trade.

Different strands or genres of growth models have proliferated. In the endogenous growth theory à la Lucas (1995) and Romer (1990), the role of innovation and knowledge-creation processes in generating growth via R&D is emphasized. Readers may consult Aghion and Howitt (2008), Helpman (2004), Lucas (2003) and Solow (2000) for a detailed overview.

Growth theoretic models in macroeconomics considering the role of trade have emphasized the role of global integration for innovation, diffusion and technological spillovers as well as trade costs. See, for example, Acemoglu and Azar (2020), Buera and Oberfield (2020), Coe and Helpman (1995), Coe, Helpman and Hoffmaister (1997), Eaton and Kortum (1999), Grossman and Helpman (1991a), Keller (2000), Navaretti and Tarr (2000) and Rivera-Batiz and Romer (1991).

Most of these papers focus on how trade leads to flow of ideas, transmission of knowledge, and how knowledge accumulation translates into IRS via positive external spillovers. More importantly, avoiding diminishing returns to capital accumulation for sustained growth via technology creation, human capital and institutions is crucial (Acemoglu and Ventura [2002], Lucas [2003, 2009a, 2009b]). In some models, the role of trade and transport costs for global diffusion of ideas is discussed to show strong complementarities between changes in trade costs and in the arrival rates of ideas (see Buera and Oberfield [2020] for further details). In a recent paper, Melitz and Redding (2021) attributed static and dynamic welfare gains to market size, competition, comparative advantage and knowledge spillover, as well as trade affecting growth endogenously; they also highlighted the necessity of exploring "alternative mechanisms" for achieving dynamic welfare gains from trade.

The continued global integration of trade and FDI is having an impact on income and wage inequality. In all these models, the impact on factor income – skilled workers, unskilled workers, return to capital or land – has also gained attention. These models also explore the forces – broadly speaking, trade versus technology – causing such impacts (see Chusseau, Dumont and Hellier [2008], Kurokawa [2012], Rodrik [2021] and Wang, Findlay and Thangavelu [2021]). Rodrik [2021] discusses the current situation to emphasize the redistribution aspect (apart from gains from trade) raising concern that deep integration could have ambiguous effects. A wide range of studies has explored the relationship between trade and wage inequality on both theoretical and empirical fronts. The mixed evidence on the empirical front is too voluminous to report here. Interested readers can see surveys such as Catão and Obstfeld (2019), Kosters (1994), Krugman (2008) and Pavcnik (2019). Krugman and Lawrence (1994) attributed this inequality to SBTC, while Furusawa, Konishi and Anh Tran (2019), Krugman (2008), Richardson (1995) and Wood (1994) have found recent evidence on trade increasing the wage gap. Pavcnik (2019) and Wood (1994) conclude that for developing countries the trade impact on wage inequality is more nuanced but having spillover effects on educational attainment and skill factor. On a theoretical angle, Jones and Marjit (1995), Marjit (2008) and Marjit and Kar (2013, 2018), based on the Jonesian paradigm (e.g., Jones [1965, 1971, 2018] and Markusen [2021]), have studied such aspects via providing a mechanism based on different factor intensities or factor shares, which are general equilibrium in nature. Based on these, we can say that depending on factor intensities, and the share of capital or labor types in cost, wage inequality aggravates or improves. Trade and technology both play important roles, especially with more outsourcing (see Autor, Katz and Krueger [1998], Berman, Bound and Machlin [1998], Blum [2008] and Zeira [2007]). However, it is necessary to highlight the importance of falling communication costs, aside from decline in transport costs and elimination of trade barriers. This helps in exploring whether the rise in inequality in emerging economies is due to labor-linking technology.

From the preceding discussion, we see that especially after the emergence of ICT and other technologies shaping the contours of interconnectedness, trade in virtual platforms has been a dominant force for global integration. Problems of sustainability of growth with unfolding of VT depend on consideration of TZ-based differences as well as a constellation of factors such as skill endowments of workers along with ICT infrastructure, among others. Hence, trade is a necessary but not sufficient driver for economic growth to happen on a sustained basis. Lucas (2003) also mentions that – as opposed to traditional trade-led growth arguments – elimination of trade barriers will not necessarily translate into automatic economic growth because trade's efficient resource allocation effects need to be coupled with an increase in investment rate (say in physical capital, human capital-induced skill and creativity). Further, to quote Lucas (2003, pp. 7–8, 9): "[C]lassic trade theory does not really help in understanding the connections between trade and growth that we see in the post-war period. [But] the evidence on trade and growth suggests that the rate of diffusion of technology depends on economic interactions—on trade." In fact, Lucas and Moll (2014) pointed out the deficiency of "exogenous" or "endogenous" growth theory for ignoring the *time allocation* for interactions that could shape long-run growth and income distribution. This is further corroborated by a proliferation of research along the lines of Catão and Obstfeld (2019), Das (2015), Das and Drine (2020), Keller (2004), Lucas (1988), Rivera-Batiz and Romer (1991), Rodrik (2017), Romer (1994) and Stiglitz and Greenwald (2014). As mentioned in the macro-growth literature, skill and education, and structural transformation from low- to high-productivity activities as well as trade policy play very crucial roles in harnessing the benefits of trade as a vehicle for technical progress (Buera and Lucas [2018], Lucas and Moll [2014], Rodrik [2017]). Workhorse models of trade–growth linkages with a clearly spelled-out mechanism of efficient utilization of the benefits of ICT-enabled virtual platforms in intermediate input across NOLTZs are rare. In a recent study, Duernecker, Meyer, and Vega-Redondo (2021) showed that beyond the typical traditional measure of country openness, the trade–growth nexus is further strengthened by the widespread world trade network.

As mentioned elsewhere, economic growth by itself is a *time-varying* process, and technical progress is knowledge and know-how embodied in objects, that is, products that grow over time and cause information to grow. Growth of information networks among economic actors facilitates technological progress, accumulation of knowledge, and its transmission via more interactions and communications. Time is a significant factor here. For example, the role of time in determining shift-work as well as leisure-work choices is crucial. Morton (2006, p. 68) opined: "The internet is one of the most important innovations of the 20th century. Websites that make traditional sales generate consumer surplus through availability, variety and convenience to the consumer. [The Internet] allows consumers to quickly and easily gather price information from a variety of sellers … [and] save[s] consumers time [o]n mundane tasks." In fact, unlike the New Trade Theory literature, where variety-seeking individuals' "love for variety" generates trade, here *love for timely consumption* or a *preference for instant gratification* along with ICT boons work jointly to facilitate organizing such production in stages to economize on time.

Time is irreversible and information grows over time to create knowledge, which causes economic growth through large productive networks of human beings (Hidalgo [2015]). However, the standard trade–innovation–growth literature fails to consider how VT opens windows of opportunity and causes large-scale variations in economic activities in a potentially profitable way. The fourth dimension of trade based on TZs adds a new dimension to the growth mechanism in addition to the conventional factors. With VT based on ICT, we see this additional factor causing "imported intermediate-input augmenting or value-added augmenting technical change" via fragmentation of the stages of production. Through *dual effects* – time-saving as well as quality – further growth occurs, ultimately resulting in permanent growth via improvement in productivity by dint of effective utilization of TZs. While flourishing online transactions are gaining prominence, this could be a new force for growth with spillovers of benefits across nations.

Three interrelated key factors are:

(i) *delivery timeliness* – the role of timely delivery to avoid delivery lag or delay;

(ii) *consumption timeliness* – consumers' preference for timely delivery as they discount delayed consumption and the value of consumption falls with untimely availability;

(iii) *exploitation of TZ cycle* – utilization of the day–night cycle across NOLTZs to reduce by half the usual twenty-four-hour production cycle. Of course, trade in intermediate business services that makes such utilization beneficial is possible only due to advancements in ICT. As mentioned before, the global revolution in the ICT and 4IR starting from the latter half of the twentieth century led to nosedived communication costs as well as *time-saving and trade-augmenting technical progress.* As mentioned in Sections 1 and 2, key differences are attributed to four interlinked factors:

   (i) *technology network effects* – reduction in costs of delay or iceberg effect;

  (ii) *trade-induced innovation and TOT effects* – increase in output and marginal productivity of capital in both nations, increasing the capital stock;

 (iii) *efficient resource allocation effects* – via intermediate inputs usage;

 (iv) *investment rate effects.*

The traditional literature emphasizing the growth effects of trade did not consider internalizing such time-preference for consumption as a driving force for organizing trade. This fourth dimension of trade makes Adam Smith's notion of division of labor and specialization-based growth much wider and broader via incorporating a natural-time endowment-based division of the life cycle of a product into the production process. Thus, it has much potential to have a growth-generating effect. In fact, Aghion, Antonin and Bunel (2021) have analyzed that after the recent pandemic disrupted jobs and pushed large numbers of firms out of business, a process of *creative destruction* via online trade and commerce has been initiated. This can easily be a lever of growth via virtual activities and new online trade that are efficient and more responsive to the needs of consumers. Thus, the virtues of such trade were more vivid during confinement under the COVID-19 crisis when VT could promote growth in a new and innovative way. Such trade causes a fall in the costs of service links, favoring fragmentation of production.

    This is unlike the traditional literature where the transmission mechanism is entirely different. We will see that if we consider such TZ interface between developed Home (destination) and developing countries (source of imported intermediates), then faster growth in the developing economies is warranted with improved TOT in the latter. In fact, this could be a force for inclusive growth on a sustained basis as developing countries take up the opportunities brought about by declining costs of service-led production links (Jones and Marjit [2001]).[29] Also, the level effect versus the growth effect of such a trade mechanism is of considerable interest (Marjit, Mandal and Nakanishi [2020]). Continuity and synchronization effects are important here for organizing TZ-based trade. Why? This is simply because, with TZ effects, trade emerges between NOLTZs to take advantage of day and night work-shifts in, say, the USA, the UK and India or China, while workers differ in terms of their preferences for leisure–labor as well as splitting work hours between day and nighttime work.[30] All these depend on individual utilities, relative degrees of aversion to sacrificing resting time, and human capital differences. For example, in Sections 3.4 and 3.5, using specific-labor skill types and a mobile capital–augmented general equilibrium trade model, we show that a reduction in communication costs along with utilization of TZ differences could increase the wage gap between skilled and unskilled workers. This primarily happens as outsourcing of services raises demand for educational capital. For complementary factors of production, unskilled wage rises compared to rental on capital because the production process is less intensive in capital. While trade leads to a one-shot jump in real income, the mechanism for growth as embedded in the process of international trade is sparse and not well-researched, despite there being available voluminous empirical evidence.

3.3 A Model of Time Zone Differences–Induced Growth

In this section, we present a representative model based on the prototypical AK model familiar in modern growth theory literature where this "time-element" is incorporated to show how organizing intermediate business services across separate TZs could generate productivity growth by reducing time-cost.[31] As mentioned in Section 3.1, the basic ingredient is timely delivery to reduce costs of delay as consumers value time. Thus, ICT networks induce a mutually reinforcing time-saving (via quick delivery) and trade-augmenting (via low shipping costs for imported business services) effect (acceleration of production).

---

[29] Precisely speaking, inclusive growth ensures economic growth that automatically ensures fair distribution across societies and ensures opportunities for all. If TZ-induced trade translates into reducing inequality both within and across countries in addition to the improved TOT for developing countries, this would surely address the main pillars of inclusive growth in the developing part of the globe, which is by definition deprived of various opportunities.

[30] In a finer sense, TZ-differences-induced impact on growth may also be viewed as an impact on growth due to increase in productivity owing to the fact that trade is driven by differences in TZs.

[31] In neoclassical growth models, several types of technical progress are theorized. See, for example, Barro and Sala-i-Martin (1995) for "AK" (where A = technology and K = capital).

Following Acemoglu and Ventura (2002), we present a simple two-country AK model of intermediate services trade along with the role of TZ differences.[32] Home and Foreign countries are located in different TZs without overlap in working hours. The key assumption is that domestic business-services production requires only one workday and the product is ready for sale after one workday. Hence, the delivery of domestic business services involves significant costs in terms of delay, while utilization of communications networks allows production in a foreign country where nonoverlapping work hours and business-services trade via networks enable quick delivery. Thus, imported services whose production benefits from TZ differences provide higher value than domestically produced services. This assumption is at odds with the conventional trade models with trade costs.[33] Based on such arguments, we establish that an acceleration in intermediate business-services trade may have a permanent impact on productivity.

Let us assume that when Home's daytime working hours end, daytime working hours in Foreign begin. In Home, the final good, Y, and the Home intermediate business services, X, are both produced under perfect competition. The final good is produced with capital, K, domestically provided intermediate business services, X, and Foreign-produced intermediate business services, $\widetilde{X}$, via:

$$Y = AK^{\alpha}(X)^{\frac{(1-a)}{2}}(\widetilde{X})^{\frac{(1-a)}{2}}. \tag{60}$$

Only intermediate business services are traded. The final good and capital are not traded. One unit of intermediate business service is required to produce one unit of the final good, Y. The key assumption is that time-cost for the delivery of intermediates is important. In order to capture this point, we assume that shipments of intermediates incur the iceberg effect of delivery costs: to sell one unit of foreign intermediates in Home, $\widetilde{t}$ units must be shipped. Note that $\widetilde{t} > 1$. We can interpret $\widetilde{t}$ as a measure of the inverse of the delivery timeliness: a lower value of $\widetilde{t}$ implies a quicker delivery. Domestically produced "intermediates" are ready for sale after one workday, whereas imported intermediates whose production benefits from TZ differences are available sooner. To parameterize the timing of delivery, we treat the utilization of communications networks as a reduction in the delivery time of imported intermediates. Let us denote the Foreign intermediates' delivery timeliness before technological change as $\widetilde{t}^{1}$ and that after change as $\widetilde{t}^{2}$. Therefore,

---

[32] Aghion and Howitt (2008) discussed the implications of a two-country version of the AK model.

[33] Based on a model of economic geography, Harrigan and Venables (2006) argue that when the stages of the value chain are physically separated, it takes more time to complete a project. Contrary to that, we argue that it takes less time to complete a project if utilizing TZ differentials.

$$\tilde{t}^1 > 1 > \tilde{t}^2. \tag{61}$$

Consider the final good, Y, as the numeraire. Since markets are perfectly competitive, the price of Home intermediates, X, is equal to their unit cost; thus, it is also equal to one. In contrast to this, the price of Foreign intermediate business services is given by $\tilde{p}$. Given these assumptions, the optimal X and $\tilde{X}$ maximize final-sector profits:

$$K^{\alpha}(X)^{\frac{(1-\alpha)}{2}}\left(\tilde{X}\right)^{\frac{(1-\alpha)}{2}} - X - \tilde{t}\tilde{p}\tilde{X}.$$

The first-order conditions for profit maximization are: $X = \frac{(1-\alpha)}{2} Y$; and $\tilde{t}\tilde{p}\tilde{X} = \frac{(1-\alpha)}{2} Y$.

Thus, we obtain:

$$Y = \left(\tilde{t}\tilde{p}\right)^{-\frac{(1-\alpha)}{2\alpha}}\left(\frac{(1-\alpha)}{2}\right)^{\frac{(1-\alpha)}{\alpha}} K. \tag{62}$$

It is apparent that, though the production function (Equation [60]) has a diminishing marginal product of capital, we still have an AK model, with $Y = AK$, where the marginal product of capital, A, is given by:

$$A = \left(\tilde{t}\tilde{p}\right)^{-\frac{(1-\alpha)}{2\alpha}}\left(\frac{(1-\alpha)}{2}\right)^{\frac{(1-\alpha)}{\alpha}}. \tag{63}$$

Let us further assume a constant saving rate so that we can obtain the capital accumulation equation, namely, $\dot{K} = sY - \delta K$. Here, s is the savings rate and δ is the rate of depreciation. So, Home's growth rate depends positively on its saving rate, according to $\dot{K}/K = sA - \delta$.

Now, consider the Foreign economy with production function for the final good being:

$$Y_f = K_f^{\alpha}\left(X_f\right)^{\frac{(1-\alpha)}{2}}\left(\tilde{X}_f\right)^{\frac{(1-\alpha)}{2}}. \tag{64}$$

Suppose that $\tilde{t}_f$ measures the inverse of the delivery timeliness of Home intermediates in the foreign market, where $\tilde{t}_f\tilde{X}_f$ is given by:

$$\frac{1}{\tilde{p}}\tilde{t}_f\tilde{X}_f = \frac{(1-\alpha)}{2} Y_f. \tag{65}$$

By analogy to Equation (62) we have:

$$Y_f = \left(\tilde{t}_f\right)^{\frac{(1-a)}{2a}} \left(\tilde{p}\right)^{\frac{(1-a)}{2a}} \left(\frac{1-\alpha}{2}\right)^{\frac{(1-a)}{a}} K_f. \tag{66}$$

In the same way as for Home, Foreign's production function becomes $Y_f = A_f K_f$ where the marginal product of capital, A_f, is given by:

$$A_f = \left(\tilde{t}_f\right)^{\frac{(1-a)}{2a}} \left(\tilde{p}\right)^{\frac{(1-a)}{2a}} \left(\frac{1-\alpha}{2}\right)^{\frac{(1-a)}{a}}. \tag{67}$$

From Equations (65) and (66):

$$\tilde{t}_f \tilde{X}_f = \left(\tilde{t}_f\right)^{\frac{(1-a)}{2a}} \left(\tilde{p}\right)^{\frac{(1+a)}{2a}} \left(\frac{1-\alpha}{2}\right)^{\frac{1}{a}} K_f. \tag{68}$$

From the Home export's value condition $\left(\tilde{t}\tilde{p}\tilde{X}\right)$, we have:

$$\tilde{t}\tilde{p}\tilde{X} = \left(\tilde{t}\tilde{p}\right)^{-\frac{(1-a)}{2a}} \left(\frac{1-\alpha}{2}\right)^{\frac{1}{a}} K. \tag{69}$$

Trade balance implies that $\tilde{t}\tilde{p}\tilde{X} = \tilde{t}_f \tilde{X}_f$ holds. Then, from Equations (68) and (69), we solve for the equilibrium relative price of foreign intermediates:

$$\tilde{p} = \left(\frac{\tilde{t}_f}{\tilde{t}}\right)^{\frac{1-a}{2}} K^a \tag{70}$$

where k is the relative capital stock: $k \equiv \frac{K}{K_f}$.

Now let us consider the steady state. From Home's growth equation,

$$\dot{K}/K = s\left(\tilde{t}\tilde{p}\right)^{-\frac{(1-a)}{2a}} \left(\frac{1-\alpha}{2}\right)^{\frac{(1-a)}{a}} - \delta$$

$$= s\left(\frac{1-\alpha}{2}\right)^{\frac{(1-a)}{a}} \left(\tilde{t}\right)^{-\frac{(1-a^2)}{4a}} \left(\tilde{t}_f\right)^{-\frac{(1-a)^2}{4a}} (k)^{-\frac{(1-a)}{2}} - \delta. \tag{71}$$

And from the growth equation of the foreign country, we derive:

$$K_f/K_f = s_f \left(\frac{\tilde{p}}{\tilde{t}_f}\right)^{\frac{(1-a)}{2a}} \left(\frac{1-\alpha}{2}\right)^{\frac{(1-a)}{a}} - \delta$$

$$= s_f \left(\frac{1-\alpha}{2}\right)^{\frac{(1-a)}{a}} \left(\tilde{t}\right)^{-\frac{(1-a)^2}{4a}} \left(\tilde{t}_f\right)^{-\frac{(1-a^2)}{4a}} (k)^{\frac{(1-a)}{2}} - \delta. \tag{72}$$

It follows that the growth rate of the relative capital stock, k, is just the differential growth rate $\dot{K}/K - \dot{K}_f/K_f$. Therefore, Equations (71) and (72) yield:

$$\dot{k}/k = \left(\frac{1-\alpha}{2}\right)^{\frac{(1-\alpha)}{\alpha}}$$

$$\left[s(\widetilde{t})^{-\frac{(1-\alpha^2)}{4\alpha}}(\widetilde{t}_f)^{-\frac{(1-\alpha)^2}{4\alpha}}(k)^{-\frac{(1-\alpha)}{2}} - s_f(\widetilde{t})^{-\frac{(1-\alpha)^2}{4\alpha}}(\widetilde{t}_f)^{-\frac{(1-\alpha^2)}{4\alpha}}(k)^{\frac{(1-\alpha)}{2}}\right].$$

(73)

This is a stable, ordinary differential equation with the unique steady state:

$$k^* = \left(\frac{s}{s_f}\right)^{\frac{1}{1-\alpha}}\left(\frac{\widetilde{t}_f}{\widetilde{t}}\right)^{\frac{1}{2}}$$

(74)

where an asterisk indicates the steady-state value of a variable. Substituting this into Equation (70), we obtain the steady-state-relative price of foreign intermediates:

$$\widetilde{p}^* = \left(\frac{s}{s_f}\right)^{\frac{\alpha}{1-\alpha}}\left(\frac{\widetilde{t}_f}{\widetilde{t}}\right)^{\frac{1}{2}}.$$

(75)

Using Equations (74), (75), (63) and (67) one gets the steady-state marginal productivity of capital:

$$A^* = \left(\frac{s_f}{s}\right)^{\frac{1}{2}}(\widetilde{t}\,\widetilde{t}_f)^{-\frac{(1-\alpha)}{4\alpha}};$$

(76)

$$A_f{}^* = \left(\frac{s}{s_f}\right)^{\frac{1}{2}}(\widetilde{t}\,\widetilde{t}_f)^{-\frac{(1-\alpha)}{4\alpha}}.$$

(77)

To show the impact of utilization of TZ differences on trade, we now consider the impact of a time-saving technological advancement in communications captured by a reduction in *one country's* delivery cost. Suppose that the value of $\widetilde{t}$ decreases from $\widetilde{t}^1$ to $\widetilde{t}^2$ in Equation (61), while $\widetilde{t}_f$ remains unchanged. This implies that the final good producers in Home can access $\widetilde{X}$ more quickly. It can be shown that in the new steady state both countries experience an increase in the marginal productivity of capital at the *same rate*. To be more precise: from Equation (63), a lower $\widetilde{t}$ will cause faster capital-stock growth in Home. Since Home final good producers use imported Foreign intermediates with quicker access, the demand for them rises. On the contrary, the Foreign demand for Home intermediates, $\widetilde{X}_f$, will not grow as fast as the Home demand for Foreign intermediates. Thus, $\widetilde{p}$ must increase to preserve the trade balance. This TOT effect will tend to bring Home's growth rate down (Acemoglu and Ventura [2002]). In Foreign, this TOT improvement triggers faster capital-stock growth via changes in the TOT. The effect of one country's technological improvement is transmitted to the other country. This effect stabilizes world growth: growth rates of K and K_f will move toward each other.

Our result suggests that one country's time-saving technological improvement, which induces firms to take advantage of TZ differences based on natural comparative advantage, will also boost the other country's *permanent growth or permanent increase in productivity.* Here, with an exogenous saving rate and fixed technology level, there is absence of diminishing returns to capital (average product of capital is equal to marginal product of capital here). Long-run growth occurs here via TOT effects with more trade in intermediate services due to cost reduction. This works like an improvement in the level of technology inducing productivity spillovers via greater accumulation of capital. Indirectly, the potential for endogenous technical change occurs via reduction in trade costs and avoiding delays in consumption. In the next section, we go beyond this level effect to a model where VT could have a positive direct impact on growth rates of trade partners due to increase in both investment rate and per unit time.

3.4 A Model of Separated Time-Zone-Induced Optimal Growth Through Virtual Trade

We may use the idea of VT in intermediates induced by NOLTZs to show how trade increases the equilibrium optimal rate of growth. Unlike the model in Section 3.3, we need to consider a framework of endogenous growth with skill accumulation to sustain the growth permanently where wage rate rises and remains unaltered in the long run. The mechanism is entirely different from typical neoclassical literature. Also, one can incorporate production taking place in double shifts with lower costs without nightly production. Typically, nightly wage being costly, a twelve-hour work cycle is used for each input, and this causes earlier production as well as more output given the time frame and cost (see Marjit, Mandal and Nakanishi [2020]). Here, daytime vis-à-vis night-shift wage differences as well as differences in wages across nations matter along with the novelty of the VT mechanism in producing intermediates over NOLTZs to reduce inefficiency beyond typical resource allocation effects.

Here we consider two symmetric countries, identical in all respects but located in two different NOLTZs. Therefore, autarkic equilibrium in one will be replicated in another. We have a single final good, Y, which uses capital, K, and intermediates, m_1 and m_2, and they need two twelve-hour cycles to be produced. One unit of Y is produced by one unit of m_1 and m_2 each. Also, we choose Y as the numeraire. Hence, all prices are unity. We rule out nightly production. So, m_1, m_2 and K are used to produce Y via the following production function. Assume that K is costless, so that, as in Section 2, we write:

$$Y = Am_1^{\frac{1-a}{2}} m_2^{\frac{1-a}{2}} K^\alpha. \tag{78}$$

Since m_1 is available only in the first half of tomorrow, and it requires another input, namely, m_2, Y cannot be delivered early and/or there may be carryover costs of m_1 up to m_2. We take up the second interpretation, although the first has been dealt with in Marjit (2007). The delay or carryover cost is denoted by $(1 + \mu)$ with $\mu > 0$ denoting a premium over unit cost.

Optimal m_1 and m_2 are given by $m_{10} = \frac{1-a}{2(1+\mu)} Y$ and $m_{20} = \frac{1-a}{2} Y$. Substituting these values in Equation (78) we get:

$$Y_0 = A^{\frac{1}{a}} \left(\frac{1-\alpha}{2} \right)^{\frac{1-a}{a}} \cdot \left[\frac{1}{(1+\mu)} \right]^{\frac{1-a}{2a}} . K \tag{79}$$

where K is aggregate capital.

Given K and other parameters, Equations (78) and (79) determine Y_0. From Equation (79) it is obvious that μ has a negative implication due to delay of delivery. Also remember that we are talking of VT through a computerized network. This may entail some trading costs, say, τ. So, the effective price of the intermediate service is $(1 + \tau)$ even if we assume away any "delay or carryover cost." So long as $\tau < \mu$, the home country will import m_2 from the foreign country and the foreign country will import m_1 from the home country.

If we work with the delay in delivery of the final good as in Marjit (2007) and the discount rate applied is $\delta(< 1)$ on the price of Y, then $m_1 = m_2 = \frac{1-a}{2} . \delta y.$[34] Thus, in the end international trade, by reducing delay in the production process, has a positive impact on productivity and growth. Note that both μ and δ must be compared with τ. If τ is very high, the growth rate must suffer. Hence, trade not only raises the value of output but also brings it onto a higher growth path.[35]

3.5 Time Zone Differences, Service Trade and Implications for Factor Prices

As has been mentioned before and especially in Section 3.2, the subject of trade versus technology in driving wage gaps between various labor types and its implications for factor markets in general has received much attention, with important contributions analyzing the consequences of such changes. However,

---

[34] See Kikuchi, Marjit and Mandal (2013), Marjit (2007) and Marjit, Mandal and Nakanishi (2020) for further explanation.

[35] We can also introduce a labor market into the model as such VT is mainly driven by the presence of skilled labor of some sort. Therefore, VT naturally raises demand for skilled labor and hence skill formation. See Beladi, Marjit and Weiher (2011), Mandal, Marjit and Nakanishi (2015) and Marjit, Mandal and Nakanishi (2020) on this issue.

based on the preceding section, we can infer that as VT in skill-intensive intermediate services also leads to growth in demand for human capital, it is a prerequisite for such trade to happen. Accumulation of skill is necessary for level and growth effects with concomitant one-time rise in real wage maintained in the steady-state growth path. First, virtual labor mobility is aided by communication network technology where it is organized in two *successive* stages with a continuation effect (*no interruptions*) of round-the-clock production (*time-reduction aspect*). Second, *reduction of reliance on shift-work* (elimination of shift-work) is possible where there are wage differentials (nighttime premium) across day and night shifts, the latter being usually higher under communications autarky. However, as the positive continuation effect dominates the negative effect of stage-synchronization in the case of the services trade, reaping the beneficial impacts of virtual labor mobility (moving away from communication autarky) will have an impact on returns to labor and capital (see Sections 1 and 2) depending on the sizes of countries.

Differing from other contemporary models with fragmentation, offshoring and trade in tasks, Marjit, Mandal and Nakanishi (2020) offers important insights where country size plays an important role. The authors extend the Jones (1971) specific-factor framework with VT-features, distinguished between capital used in shift-work industry and daytime-only industry, and consider homogeneous land and labor with heterogeneous preferences for daytime shift-work. In particular, they show that with technical progress in ICT communication networks: (i) with identical sizes, despite NOLTZs, the night-shift wage premium disappears with virtual imports of daytime labor replacing nighttime requirement, factor prices are equalized with same wages irrespective of shift-work hours, and rental rate on capital rises; (ii) output expands for the shift-work sector connected by networks. Wages for night-shift workers are higher than those for daytime shift workers in larger countries, while the reverse is true in smaller countries so that no local workers work at night there; instead, they import virtual night-shift labor services from larger countries. In this kind of extension, the degree of night-shift aversion and the consumption level of workers adjusted to real wages are important for "switching" between dual shifts, with some workers indifferent as to what shifts they work.

However, in this case capital rentals are equalized only while returns to land and labor are not equalized. Returns to landowners surely fall in smaller countries. Overall, pairs of connected countries engage in virtual labor–trade and with identical endowments – despite TZ gaps – would have comparative advantage in the shift-working commodity; thus, technological advancement would result in rise in daytime wage, fall in nighttime wage and decline in land rent. With free trade in labor services, wage rates converge with the disappearance of premium. Further extension, as outlined in Marjit, Mandal and Nakanishi (2020), with skilled and unskilled or middle-skilled workers, shows that free trade in middle-skilled labor services increases wage inequality as the skilled-intensive sector expands with such trade.

All these adjustments speak volumes for the distributional impacts of TZ-related trade through differential impacts across land, labor and capital. Such changes take place through various channels of shift-work and communication network-augmented trade expansion. In what follows, we will show a mechanism in a model where VT will cause shifts in the relative demand and supply of skilled workers and a rise in aggregate income. With other categories of labor taking part in production, we can envisage a similar mechanism but with some differences in the extent of impact.[36] Based on casual empiricism, we know that time-saving technological improvement may trigger a series of events leading to a country-wide decline in night-shift work.[37] Now we illustrate, with a simple trade model, how a time-saving improvement in business-services trade benefiting from differences in TZs can have an impact on factor markets and factor prices.

Consider two small open economies, Home and Foreign, and the ROW. All of them are endowed with skilled and unskilled labor. They produce a knowledge-intensive good X and the traditional good Y. Then, P_X and P_Y are determined in the ROW and are beyond the control of the countries we are dealing with. Markets are competitive and open every twenty-four hours. The central assumption is that one day (twenty-four hours) is divided into *two periods*: day-shift working hours and night-shift working hours, each having twelve hours. Home and Foreign are located in different TZs and there is no overlap: when Home's day-shift working hours end, Foreign's day-shift working hours begin. Except for TZ differences, these two countries are identical in terms of technology and factor endowments.

Production of Y is instantaneous in the sense that one unit of Y can be produced within day-shift working hours. The Y sector is a competitive constant returns industry using unskilled and skilled labor, with a production function:

$$Y = F(L, S_Y) \tag{80}$$

where L is the total unskilled labor, while S_Y denotes the employment of skilled labor in Y. The production of the knowledge-intensive good X necessarily involves

---

[36] A notable exception is Matsuoka and Fukushima (2010).

[37] For example, Hamermesh (1999) found a sharp decline in the proportion of evening and night work in the USA over the last twenty years. Here it is noteworthy that in developing countries like India, still we find night-shift offices working in parallel with the USA's day shift. See chapter 9 of Marjit, Mandal and Nakanishi (2020).

two stages. Thus, to produce X, skilled labor has to be used for two consecutive periods, that is, for two shifts of twelve hours each. At the end of the first period, some goods or services-in-process are obtained and additional labor is applied to process in the second period. As noted above, the key assumption is that each day is divided into two periods. Thus, if a producer of X utilizes day-shift and night-shift skilled labor continuously, a whole day is required for the preparation.

Now, let us consider the autarkic equilibrium conditions without the facility of communications networks. The technology of the knowledge-intensive good X is simplified by assuming that at each stage only one unit of skilled labor is used. We assume that each skilled worker has to choose whether they want to be employed for day-shift work or night-shift work. To establish intra-day wage differences for skilled labor, we put the following condition:

$$v^N = (1 + \theta)v^D, \theta \geq 0 \tag{81}$$

where v^D implies wage rate for day-shift work, v^N implies the same for night-shift work, and the exogenously given θ reflects the degree of dissatisfaction from night-shift work.[38]

Hence:

$$v^N \geq v^D.$$

The equality sign will hold if $\theta = 0$ implying no premium for night-shift work. This phenomenon is typical in a job market. People do not generally prefer working at night because of several reasons (see Eels [1956], Kostiuk [1990] and Lanfranchi, Ohlsson and Skalli [2002] for details). Hence, a higher wage rate acts as a booster to induce people to work at night. The return to skilled labor is denoted by:

$$v^D = P_Y F_S(L, S_Y).^{[39]} \tag{82}$$

On the other hand, X uses only skilled labor with a constant productivity $\left(\frac{1}{2+\theta}\right)$ implying a flat labor demand function. Therefore, v^D in X is determined as:

$$v^D = \frac{P_X}{2 + \theta}. \tag{83}$$

Equations (82) and (83) determine the equilibrium allocation of S_Y following:

---

[38] Hamermesh (1999) developed a model in which the value of positive θ is endogenously determined for workers' undesirable hours.

[39] Unskilled wage $W = P_Y F_L(L, S_Y)$.

$$\frac{P_X}{P_Y} = \frac{F_S(L, S_Y)}{\left(\frac{1}{2+\theta}\right)}. \tag{84}$$

Again, factor market clearing requires that:

$$S_X^D + S_X^N + S_Y = S \tag{85}$$

where S_X^D (respectively S_X^N) is the employment level of day (respectively, night) shift S in X, and S is the total endowment of skilled labor.

Note that in equilibrium the day-shift wage rate in the X sector should be equal to the wage rate for (day-shift) skilled labor in Y because of free mobility. To produce one unit of X, both one unit of day-shift skilled labor service and one unit of night-shift skilled labor service must be applied. The unit cost of the good X under communication autarky is (where C_{AUT} represents cost in communication autarky):

$$C_{AUT} = v^N + v^D;$$

$$C_{AUT} = (2 + \theta)v^D. \tag{86}$$

Since X is produced in a competitive market:

$$P_X = C_{AUT} = (2 + \theta)v^D. \tag{87}$$

However, the question that naturally arises is: why does not the economy or sector X try to avoid the dissatisfaction arising from night-shift work? This requires waiting and storing the half-finished product until next day. This is called the *idle night organization mode* of production, and it attracts some extra cost in the form of *waiting decay* or *storage cost*. This is in line with Marjit (2007). This extra cost is denoted by r (per diem), which must be borne by the producers since workers need to be paid v^D as their daily wage. Labor will not work at any wage less than v^D since it is an "outside option." On the other side, "waiting decay" is a mere reflection of consumers' preference.[40] They value the product less if delivered a day later. Producers see this behavior as one where some amount of product is lost that requires to be replenished by adding some more labor cost. This is denoted by δ. Hence the zero-profit condition for X becomes

$$P_X = v^D(1 + \delta)(1 + r) + v^D(\text{where } r, \delta > 0). \tag{88}[41]$$

---

[40] For further clarification, see Marjit (2007) and Marjit, Mandal and Nakanishi (2020).

[41] See Marjit (2007) and Marjit, Mandal and Nakanishi (2020): the concern of time preference should affect the return to skilled wage on both days.

Comparing Equations (87) and (88), night-shift mode would be preferred over idle night organization mode if

$$\theta < \{\delta + (1 + \delta)r\}. \tag{89}$$

If for some reason this cost per diem (r) or δ falls significantly, producers may switch to the idle night organization mode of production.

A closer inspection of Equations (87) and (88) yields that for a closed and small economy, wage rates for skilled workers would be different under two different modes of organization. Such difference is driven by the delay cost in delivery, higher night wages, the discount factor and the cost per diem.

Under the condition in Equation (89), the skilled wage rate when night-shift mode is utilized (v_{NS}^D) is greater than the skilled wage rate when idle night organization mode is utilized (v_{IN}^D) in production.

In Figure 5 we determine the equilibrium values under communications autarky. The two vertical axes measure the wage rate for skilled labor and the horizontal axis measures the total endowment of skilled labor, S. Given the endowment of unskilled labor, we draw a downward-sloping marginal productivity schedule for skilled labor used in Y, from the left-hand origin and that in the knowledge-intensive X sector from the right-hand origin.

Let us take the traditional good Y as the numeraire and start with exogenously given P_X. Then the day-shift wage rate for skilled labor is determined from Equation (87). Given this day-shift wage rate for skilled labor, we can determine

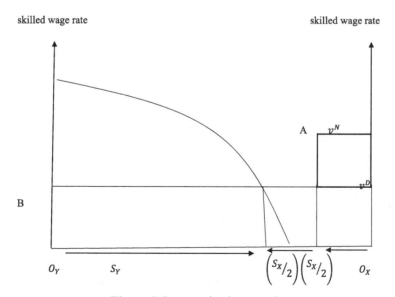

Figure 5 Communication autarky

the employment levels S_X and S_Y: $S_X/_2$ is employed as a day-shift worker while the rest $S_X/_2$ are employed as night-shift workers. The rectangle covered by bold lines indicates the total additional payments for the night-shift workers, $\theta v^D S_X^N$ (the area named $ABv^D v^N$).

In this structure, when a country is opened up for trade, another possibility comes into play. Here, we consider only those countries that are not in the same TZ as the country concerned, that is, nonoverlapping. This allows for gain through removing both dissatisfaction with night-shift work and the cost of the idle night organization mode. This, however, comes with some other costs. Realistically, we assume that vertical product sharing requires some communication cost at the rate τ (say). Here we focus only on iceberg variety communication cost.[42]

In our scenario, products-in-process at the end of one country's daytime will be sent to the other country using ICT and the day-shift skilled labor of that country will be used there. Three possible cases may arise: (a) Home specializes in the first stage while Foreign specializes in the second stage, (b) Foreign specializes in the first stage and Home specializes in the second stage, and (c) in each country, half of the workers in the X sector work in the first stage, while the rest work in the second stage. Although trade patterns are different in each case, the factor market implications are qualitatively the same. Thus, we will concentrate only on the first case (a). Taking a clue from Equation (89), vertical product sharing or vertical trade (virtual in nature) would be chosen if[43]

$$(2 + \tau) < (2 + \theta). \tag{90}$$

The skilled wage rate would be:

$$v_{NT}^D = \frac{P_X}{2 + \tau} \tag{91}$$

where $v_{NT}^D \Rightarrow$ skilled wage rate when network technology comes with cost at a rate τ.

To focus on the central point of this section, let us consider that $v_{NT}^D \left(v_{NT}^D = \frac{P_X}{2+\tau} \right) \leq v_{NS}^D \left(v_{NS}^D = \frac{P_X}{2+\theta} \right)$. Assume that technological advancement takes place in the communication network. This advancement reduces the

---

[42] The physical cost of trade due to distance is an important impediment to trade in services too. For details, see Head, Mayer and Ries (2009). An interesting reference in this connection is Marjit and Mandal (2012).

[43] In a sense, the country buying the half-finished product needs to indebt itself and hence must pay back more than the equivalent of v^D if we consider a positive interest rate. So, we may think of generalizing this model to encompass a broader notion such as half year, or season, where the idea of a positive interest rate would make more sense. Assume that $(2 + \theta) < \{(1 + \delta)(1 + r) + 1\}$ when we start from night-shift mode.

trade cost τ as well as the labor cost: now no country needs to utilize night-shift workers where the cost of production becomes higher. In this case, since technology is identical among countries, the same day-shift wage rate $\tilde{v}^D$ will be applied twice along with reduced trade cost. Say the reduced trade cost is τ_1 such that $\tau_1 < \tau$. Hence, the unit cost with communication network can be written as:

$$C_{NT} = (2 + \tau_1)\tilde{v}^D \qquad (92)$$

where C_{NT} represents cost with communication network advancement.

In this case, the equilibrium wage rate for day-shift skilled workers $\tilde{v}^D$ is derived from the condition that $P_X = C_{NT}$.

Hence,

$$\tilde{v}^D = \frac{P_X}{(2 + \tau_1)}. \qquad (93)$$

If $\tau_1 < \theta$ then $\tilde{v}^D > v^D$. It is further apparent from v_{NS}^D and v_{IN}^D for a sufficiently small τ_1, $\tilde{v}_{NT}^D$ is likely to be higher than v_{NS}^D. It is interesting to note that there will be no night-shift work in the service sector.

The impact of technological advancement in this connection is represented in Figure 6, which compares the communication autarky equilibrium (point M) and the equilibrium with communication networks (point N). The impact can be interpreted as if the disutility from night-shift labor supply, θ, vanishes, whereas the advantage through reduced communication cost comes in.[44] When $\tau_1 < \theta$, this raises the day-shift skilled wage and increases the resources devoted to X: the new equilibrium is depicted as point N in Figure 6.

At the same time, the unskilled labor wages are reduced. Thus, the present model predicts an increase in the wages of day-shift skilled labor, a decrease in unskilled wages and an increase in the skill premium.[45] Sources of these changes can be divided into two: (1) switching from the night-shift work toward the day-shift work within X, and (2) intersectoral labor reallocation due to utilization of TZ differences. Further, since the night-shift work bears significant additional costs for workers, it is costly to produce X under communication autarky. Utilization of TZ differences removes these additional costs and it becomes more comfortable to work in X. This induces more skilled workers to choose and move to work in X.

---

[44] Zaheer (2000) emphasizes the productivity gains from the entrainment or synchronization of individual circadian rhythms, the social rhythms and work rhythms.

[45] Harris (1998) emphasizes this kind of labor market.

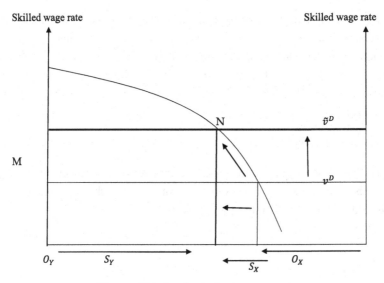

Figure 6 Technological advancement

The effect on the national income of each country is unambiguously positive if the skilled wage increases. The national income is equal to the factor income, which is given by $(wL + vS)$. We have already argued that the increase in returns to skilled labor is more than offset by the losses to unskilled labor. Thus, if trade with TZ differences raises skilled wages, it will undoubtedly raise aggregate real income and productivity.

One interesting implication of this extension is that in each country the wage ratio of skilled to unskilled workers increases, an outcome that has eluded the standard HOS model. Interesting work on two-sided wage inequality in both the North and the South includes Davis (1998), Feenstra and Hanson (1996), Marjit and Acharyya (2006) and Marjit and Kar (2009). However, trade across TZs as a natural catalyst in the process has never been explored. It is possible that the TZ advantage could also benefit the middle-skilled.

3.6 Summary and Insights

In this section, we discussed how growth induced by VT in intermediate business services could have level and growth effects. The brief review of such issues highlighted that it is different from the traditional trade-growth nexus where the role of communication networks facilitating TZ-based trade is set aside. Furthermore, we analyzed that skill-intensive service requires accumulation of skill to augment human capital with a fixed population size.

Through separated TZs, it generates simultaneous gains from trade and growth effects, and leads to a permanent rise in productivity as production occurs round the clock for twenty-four hours with continuity effect. Without skill constraints, balanced growth will occur with the same rate of human capital accumulation and one-time increase in wage, as well as aggregate real income. With virtual labor mobility and shift-work in the daytime without nighttime work (as the night-shift wage premium is replaced by imported labor services), technological improvement in communication networks, wages and other factor prices will be equalized in cases of countries with identical size. In an extension with skilled–unskilled labor categories, time-saving technological improvement and VT affect respective wages via shifts in the relative demand and supply for skilled workers. With boons of communication networks, and lowered costs of such trade, benefits could also accrue to middle-skilled or low-skilled workers with diverse preferences for (or degrees of aversion to) night-shift and day-shift works as well as leisure–work trade-offs.

4 Capital Mobility and Virtual Trade

4.1 Introduction

By now, it will be quite evident to you, the reader, that vertical fragmentation or disintegration of production processes (and consequently offshoring or outsourcing) is not a new phenomenon and has become more pervasive, affecting the choices of exports and FDI at home and abroad.[46] In fact, it has been in the literature of international trade and industrial organizations for quite a long time. Some earlier contributions regarding trade in intermediates are Feenstra (1998, 2010), Jones (2000), Marjit (1987), Sanyal (1983) and Sanyal and Jones (1982). However, till Krugman's (1979) classic publication no one was much interested in the firm – the *black box*. Numerous papers written later, including Antràs (2003), Antràs et al. (2012) and Antràs and Helpman (2004), are also in line with Krugman (1979), although these papers do not deal with trade in intermediate or business services (see Sections 1 and 2 in this Element). That said, it does not matter whether we trade in goods or services as long as the crucial aspects of cost of production and cost of transportation are taken into account. Later the issue takes an interesting turn when cost of sending and procuring either finished or unfinished services goes down owing to various reasons along with the possibility of *continuity effect* (Kikuchi,

---

[46] In this context we wish to mention an ambitious research possibility. Availability of close to costless transfer of semifinished service-work across TZs through information communication networks may have a pretty important implication for the decision to invest in production networks in other countries. One interesting prospect against this backdrop could be goods production offshoring to countries located in the vicinity with service production outsourcing to a country located in a distant NOLTZ.

2011). Some related literature comprises Deardorff (2003), Do and Long (2008), Grossman and Rossi-Hansberg (2008), Kikuchi (2011), Kikuchi and Marjit (2011), Kikuchu, Marjit and Mandal (2013), Long, Riezman and Soubeyran (2005), Mandal (2015), Marjit (2007), Marjit, Mandal and Nakanishi (2020), Matsuoka and Fukushima (2010) and Nakanishi and Long (2015) – to name but a few. Recently, Antràs and Gortari (2020) constructed a multistage general equilibrium model to show the role of trade cost in determining production location, and proximity of location, as well as participation in value chains. The proximate cause is attributed to flourishing ICT networks and computer-aided "splitting or slicing" of the value chain into stages. Here we should note that revolution in ICT alone is not sufficient to capitalize on the cost difference between two trading partners. This phenomenon coupled with difference in TZs conjointly works to have a combined effect and meaningful impacts on volume of trade and gains from trade. Two trading partners might not be able to appropriate the difference in cost of production so effectively, even if it exists, if they are located in overlapping TZ (see discussions in Sections 1 and 2). This is perhaps where globalization and trade touch the greatest height to exploit the advantage conferred by *differences*.[47]

On a related issue concerned with international mobility of capital, in the conventional literature we observe that capital movement historically faces less restraint than physical movement of labor (or workers with distribution of talents or skill types). International mobility of homogeneous capital does occur, while specific capital cannot move so easily and readily in the short or medium run. For example, educational capital nowadays moves from developed to developing countries with rise in demand as economies develop. Scarcity of educational capital and training facilities in the developing world is the main driving force behind such mobility.

Given the above backdrop of theoretical research mixed with empiricism, here we analyze the possible consequences for factor prices and the inflow of educational capital of massive reduction in cost of ICT coupled with the advantages of TZ differences between countries.

4.2 Foreign Direct Investment and Skill Formation in the Context of Time-Zone-Differences-Induced Trade

To start with, consider two small open economies: Home (H) and Foreign (F), and the ROW. The primary focus is on the economy that outsources and/or insources *both* unfinished and finished services. Here, both H and F need to bear

---

[47] Recent literature comprises Deardorf (2003), Dixit and Grossman (1982), Do and Long (2008), Findlay (1978), Grossman and Rossi-Hansberg (2008), Jones and Kierzkowski (1990), Jones and Marjit (2001, 2009), Kikuchi (2011), Kikuchi and Marjit (2011), Kikuchi, Marjit and Mandal (2013), Kohler (2004a, 2004b), Long, Riezman and Soubeyran (2005), Marjit (1987, 2007), Sanyal (1983), Sarkar (1985).

the cost of virtual communication. Let us assume that the representative economy is endowed with skilled labor (S), unskilled labor (L) and two distinct types of capital. One kind of capital (K) is used directly for production and the other one, educational capital (E), is used for training unskilled labor. We assume E to be internationally mobile. All other factors are also mobile only across sectors, but immobile across countries. The concerned country produces three goods, namely, X, Y and Z. Of these, X is a technical sector, which requires only skilled labor (S). However, it is extremely important to note that X requires two consecutive twelve-hour working shifts, hence two units of S. Therefore, X is a vertically integrated service. The production function of X is given by $X = f(S)$. One day (twenty-four hours) is divided into *two periods*: day-shift working hours and night-shift working hours, each of twelve hours. Traditionally, wage rates are determined only for twelve hours. Markets are competitive and open every twenty-four hours. So, the country has essentially three options in regard to the production of X: (i) Half of the product/service is produced today and the rest tomorrow, with the commodity ready for sale by the morning of the third day. As the consumers prefer to get it early, there is a time-preference (Marjit [2007]).[48] (ii) Half is produced in the day-shift and the remaining half in the night-shift of the same country. Here, night workers' wages are generally higher than day wages. However, the product is ready by tomorrow morning.[49] (iii) Half is done in the daytime and then outsourced to a country located in the *NOLTZ*. The rest of the product is finished in the daytime of the other country. So, the product or service is ready tomorrow morning (morning in the first country). This is where TZ difference comes into play. With an OLTZ difference between H and F, option (iii) is meaningless. To concentrate on the issue of TZ we assume that out of these three options the third one is the best.[50] We shall start from a situation where parts of the service are produced in countries located in NOLTZs, but the cost of communication is significantly high. This will help us focus on the importance of TZ difference and cost of communication. OLTZs lead us to options (i) and (ii). Therefore, in a competitive setup with CRS technology and diminishing marginal productivity assumption, the cost–price equality for X is:

$$P_x = W_s(2 + \eta). \tag{94}$$

Here, ρ is cost of communication technology (see Marjit, Mandal and Nakanishi [2020]). Two S are used in the per unit production of X. Half is produced in, say,

---

[48] See Kikuchi (2011) and Marjit (2007) for related issues and analysis.

[49] Kikuchi, Marjit and Mandal (2013) is an important reference in this connection.

[50] If we think of outsourcing to a country where labor cost is less, our story would be further strengthened.

H and then it is sent to F at the end of the first *day* of H. F works for its "day" and finishes the final product/service. The service is sent or sent back via the Internet at a cost ηW_s. It does not matter whether η is greater or less than unity. However, we presume $0 < \eta < 1$ as communication cost per unit should not usually be more than factor cost. Further, ηW_s captures the disutility of the night-shift work or communication cost.[51]

Another commodity Y is produced by S and K and a third, Z, uses K and L. Therefore, production functions for Y and Z are respectively represented by $Y = f(S, K)$ and $Z = f(L, K)$.

We also consider another type of capital – educational capital, E. It is specifically used to upgrade L to S. All markets are competitive and, by virtue of small country assumption, goods prices are determined in the ROW. Following Jones (1965, 1971), the full employment general equilibrium condition ensures the following cost–price equality and factor market clearing conditions. The price equation for X is already mentioned in Equation (94). The same equations for Y and Z are:

$$P_y = W_s a_{sy} + r a_{ky}; \tag{95}$$

$$P_z = W a_{lz} + r a_{kz}. \tag{96}$$

Here, P_js (j=x, y, z) represents prices; a_{ij}s(i= s, k, l) indicates the technology of production; W_s is the return to skilled workers; W and r are the returns to L and capital, K, respectively. Further, as Y and Z are produced in twelve hours only (daytime), while X requires two consecutive twelve-hour periods plus the cost represented by ηW_s, a_{ij} for X is 2 and it is fixed throughout the model.

Domestic endowments of S, L and K are fixed. Competitive full employment conditions yield:

$$2X + a_{sy}Y = S + S_1 \tag{97}$$

$$a_{lz}Z = L - L_1 \tag{98}$$

$$a_{ky}Y + a_{kz}Z = K \tag{99}$$

where S_1 is newly trained or upgraded L. These laborers are originally L and thus we can assume that some L ($= L_1$) chose to be trained to be employed in

---

[51] For further details see Kikuchi, Marjit and Mandal (2013) and Marjit (2007). Here η implies only communication cost. Readers are cautioned not to confuse if η is also part of the technology of production in X; η essentially measures how much extra cost in terms of W_s is required for communication.

either Y or X. Eventually they are transformed into S_1, indicating equality between L_1 and S_1.

Upgrading L requires some cost in the form of training. It is provided by E, which is not supplied free of cost. The per unit cost of E is given by κ and μ_{ES} denotes the quantity requirement of E to upgrade one unit of L. So, in a sense S is produced by two factors, namely, L and E. The production function for S is represented as

$$S_1(E) = \varphi(E)L_1(E). \tag{100}[52]$$

Here, $\varphi(E)$ denotes a quality parameter that may capture the productivity of E over time. This idea is consistent with the literature on educational capital and human capital formation. Therefore, we assume $\varphi(E)$ to be equal to unity as one L can be transformed into one S only. Thus, the productivity of E becomes:

$$\frac{1}{\mu_{ES}} = \frac{S_1(E)}{E} = \frac{\varphi(E)L_1(E)}{E} = \frac{1}{\alpha(E)}. \tag{101}$$

Differentiating Equation (100), we get:

$$S_1'(E) = \varphi'(E)L_1(E) + L_1'(E)\varphi(E).$$

A greater supply of E indicates that more L can be upgraded to S, that is, $L_1'(E) > 0$. Even if $\varphi(E)$ is assumed to be constant, $S_1'(E) > 0$ as $L_1'(E) > 0$.

In what follows, the equation for skilled labor becomes:

$$W + \kappa\mu_{ES} = W_s. \tag{102}[53]$$

Notice that implications for μ_{ES} and $\alpha(E)$ are identical.

Before we enter the focal point of our analysis, we make sure that eventually return to E has to be identical across the globe. Even if κ goes up somewhere and attracts more E, it has to come down eventually to accommodate adjustments in the global market for E. As is evident from our previous analysis, $L_1'(E) > 0$. The average productivity of $E(AP_E)$ represented by $\frac{1}{\alpha(E)}$ or $\frac{1}{\mu_{ES}}$ must change (see Equation [101]) even when $\varphi(E)$ is constant by assumption. Therefore, return to E denoted by τ will also adjust.[54] This is shown as follows:

$$\tau = \frac{W_s - W}{\mu_{ES}} = \frac{W_s - W}{\alpha(E)}.$$

---

[52] We can easily call it transformation or an upgrade function.
[53] This equation helps us to know τ when W_s and W change due to any change in η. It cannot capture the effect of E on μ_{ES} and hence on κ. We will come to this issue in a moment.
[54] Here, θ_{ij} represents the value share of ith factor in jth good, and $^\wedge$ over a variable implies proportional change.

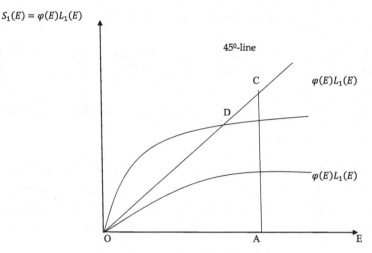

Figure 7 Average productivity of E

Therefore, $\hat{W}_s - \hat{W}\theta_{ls} = \theta_{Es}(\hat{\kappa} + \hat{\mu}_{Es})$ (103)

where, $\theta_{ls} = \frac{1.W}{W_s}$ and $\theta_{Es} = \frac{a(E).\kappa}{W_s}$.

If for some reason κ goes up, it would draw E from abroad. And hence μ_{ES} has to fall due to the fact that W_s and W do not change. This indicates a required change in AP_E with more inflow of E. Figure 7 can give us some idea about that. Note that irrespective of the position of the $\varphi(E)L_1(E)$ curve (whether it crosses the 45-degree line or not), as shown in Figure 7, our arguments hold true. Thus, $AP_E <1$ for any amount of E greater than the amount corresponding to D. To the left of D, however, we may have different implications. This indicates that AP_E should gradually fall with increasing E to guarantee international stability. The underlying arguments can also be presented in a different way. If both κ and AP_E increase simultaneously, more E will flow into the economy. This pulls up κ further. In what follows, all E will flock into the economy where κ had gone up initially and the world economy will be in a great imbalance. Desired movements of κ and E are shown in Figure 8.

Initially, return to E was κ_1 given domestic E represented by D_E and S_E. Equilibrium is determined at P. When domestic demand for E goes up to D_E', τ becomes κ_3 for any given supply of E fixed at A. Consequently, when supply slides up alongside PR, κ falls to κ_2 and equilibrium supply of E increases by AC. However, the differential in κ between this country and the ROW attracts E and S_E shifts to S_E' in such a way that the new equilibrium is attained at S, and there is no further international movement of E.

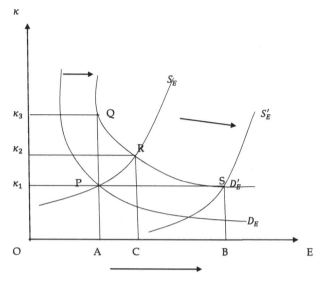

Figure 8 Return to E and supply of E

Nevertheless, if E does not change, there won't be any change in μ_{ES}. The change in κ would be triggered by and shared between W_s and W. This is shown as:

$$\hat{W}_s - \hat{W}\theta_{ls} = \theta_{Es}\hat{\kappa}. \tag{103a}$$

Now we focus on the effects of TZ differences. This is the effect of ICT revolution. The change in η will put its mark first on other factors through standard Stolper–Samuelson arguments. A reduction in η will raise W_s since the price of skilled commodity is fixed. Using conventional "hat" algebra to denote proportional change:

$$\left. \begin{aligned} \hat{W}_s &= (-)\hat{\eta}\theta_{dx} \\ \hat{r} &= \hat{\eta}\theta_{dx}\frac{\theta_{sy}}{\theta_{ky}} \\ \hat{W} &= (-)\hat{\eta}\theta_{dx}\frac{\theta_{sy}}{\theta_{ky}}\frac{\theta_{kz}}{\theta_{lz}} \end{aligned} \right\} . \tag{104[55]}$$

When η goes down, r also falls, while both skilled and unskilled labor gain. A fall in η means a decrease in communication cost. This helps S to

---

[55] Here, $\theta_{sx} = \frac{W_s(2+\eta)}{P_x} = 1$ implies productive skilled share in X, $\theta_{dx} = \frac{W_s\eta}{P_x}$ indicates communication cost share in X, and $\theta_{ky}, \theta_{sy}, \theta_{kz}, \theta_{lz}$ have the usual interpretation. See Jones (1965, 1971).

capitalize some gains. When W_s increases, the complementary factor in Y must lose. Loss to capital, K, would help L to ask for higher wages, W in Z. As both W_s and W go up, wage disparity may interestingly go either way.

$$\left(\hat{W}_s - \hat{W}\right) = (-)\hat{\eta}\theta_{dx}\left(\frac{\theta_{ky}\theta_{lz} - \theta_{sy}\theta_{kz}}{\theta_{ky}\theta_{lz}}\right) \tag{105}$$

So, wage inequality crucially hinges upon whether $\theta_{ky}\theta_{lz} \gtreqless \theta_{sy}\theta_{kz}$. Then, Y is relatively K-intensive, and Z is L-intensive. Therefore, $\theta_{ky}\theta_{lz} > \theta_{sy}\theta_{kz}$. So, wage inequality widens due to a fall in η.

Now we move to the effect on κ. This is a very important part of our analysis as E is channelized to the economy through changes in κ only. Subsequently, there would be some more changes through the Rybczynski effect. Again, when factor prices are altered, this also generates factor substitution possibility and changes in output. Change in κ without any change in endowment is shown as:

$$\hat{\kappa} = (-)\hat{\eta}\frac{\theta_{dx}}{\theta_{Es}}\left(\frac{\theta_{ky}\theta_{lz} - \theta_{sy}\theta_{kz}\theta_{ls}}{\theta_{ky}\theta_{lz}}\right). \tag{106}$$

Reasons for a rise in wage inequality were discussed before; the fact that $0 < \theta_{ls} < 1$ ensures an increase in ρ. In fact, an increase in wage inequality indicates $\hat{W}_s > \hat{W} \Rightarrow \hat{W}_s \gg \hat{W}\theta_{ls}$ as $0 < \theta_{ls} < 1 \Rightarrow \hat{\kappa} > 0$.

The underlying economic argument for low κ and low wage disparity runs as follows. Exploitation of TZ differences through the IT revolution benefits unskilled workers more than skilled workers. Thus, the incentive for L to be trained reduces and hence demand for E falls substantially in the domestic market. In an extreme situation κ may even go down and push domestic E out of the country. Consequently, the economy may end up with no training or skill upgradation. Therefore, it is not surprising to experience that the society may remain trapped in low-skilled or unskilled sectors.

Factor prices naturally determine the technology of production. Therefore, changes in factor–price ratios cause changes in the usage of factors. Exploitation of TZ difference makes this adjustment possible here. Producers start substituting among various inputs. This specifies alteration of the output combination in the basic setup. Using elasticity of substitution in Z, denoted by σ_z, we find:

$$
\left.\begin{aligned}
\hat{Z} &= (-)\hat{\eta}\sigma_z\theta_{dx}\frac{\theta_{sy}}{\theta_{ky}} > 0 \\[6pt]
\hat{Y} &= \hat{\eta}\sigma_z\theta_{dx}\frac{\theta_{sy}}{\theta_{ky}}\frac{\lambda_{kz}}{\lambda_{ky}} < 0 \\[6pt]
\hat{X} &= (-)\hat{\eta}\sigma_z\theta_{dx}\frac{\theta_{sy}}{\theta_{ky}}\frac{\lambda_{kz}}{\lambda_{ky}}\frac{\lambda_{sy}}{\lambda_{sx}} > 0
\end{aligned}\right\}. \tag{107}
$$

Here, the λs bear the usual interpretation of employment share of any factor.

While L is specific in Z, an increase in W leads to economizing on its usage. This leads to an expansion of Z for any given L. Alongside this, as Z shares the same capital with Y, this causes a contraction of Y and outflow from Y. Again, since Y shares the same S with X, released S will move to X and cause its expansion. Hence, we observe complementarity between X and Z.

As $\hat{\kappa} > 0$, some E will come in and induce further changes in the output combination of various goods. This is the standard endowment effect. The inflow of E will immediately pull some unskilled labor out of Z. This L_1 will be trained to be employed either in X or in Y, or in both. So apparently the output of Z will contract with immediate effect whereas the effects on X and Y will depend on a factor-intensity comparison between X and Y.

Equation (100) ensures that $\hat{S}_1(E) = \hat{L}_1(E)$. Hence, unskilled workers abandoned from Z and the newly trained workers awaiting employment in X and Y are identical. Thus, mathematically,

$$
\left.\begin{aligned}
\hat{Z} &= (-)\hat{E}\frac{\lambda_{l1l}}{\lambda_{lz}} < 0 \\[6pt]
\hat{Y} &= \hat{E}\frac{\lambda_{l1l}}{\lambda_{lz}}\frac{\lambda_{kz}}{\lambda_{ky}} > 0 \\[6pt]
\hat{X} &= \hat{E}\frac{\lambda_{S1S}\lambda_{lz} - \lambda_{l1l}\lambda_{kz}\lambda_{sy}}{\lambda_{lz}\lambda_{sx}}
\end{aligned}\right\} \tag{108}
$$

where $\lambda_{l1l} = \frac{L_1}{L}$; $\lambda_{lz} = \frac{a_{lz}Z}{L}$; $\lambda_{S1S} = \frac{S_1}{S}$.

Interestingly, S_1 has two alternative uses. It can be used either in X or Y or in both. However, the contraction of Z also relinquishes some K that must be employed in Y only; X does not use this. So, Y expands, and this requires some more S_1. Now the intriguing question is whether excess demand for S_1 in Y is greater or less than the newly trained S_1. This will determine the eventual effect on X. And X will increase if this condition is satisfied: $\lambda_{S1S}\lambda_{lz} > \lambda_{l1l}\lambda_{kz}\lambda_{sy}$. If the economy does not have a huge supply of S to start with, λ_{S1S} is likely to be significant, and λ_{l1l} should not be generally very high for any economy.

Therefore, $\lambda_{S1S} > \lambda_{l1l}$. On the other hand, the L intensity of Z confirms $\lambda_{lz} > \lambda_{kz}$. Therefore, $\lambda_{S1S}\lambda_{lz} > \lambda_{l1l}\lambda_{kz}\lambda_{sy}$ as $0 < \lambda_{sy} < 1$.

In what follows, both X and Y may expand simultaneously, exhibiting complementarity. The economy may end up as a skill-based one due to TZ-difference-induced inflow of E. Notably, TZ difference creates complementarity between X and Z and, in contrast, inflow of E creates complementarity between X and Y. Basically, $E = E(\kappa)$ while return to E again depends on ρ as we explained before, that is, $\kappa = \kappa(\eta)$. Therefore, $E = E(\kappa(\eta)) = g(\eta)$ (say). Tracing back the arguments established in the above analysis, it is easy to understand that $\kappa'(\eta) < 0$ whereas $E'(\kappa) > 0$. If we take the final expression for E as $E = g(\eta)$; $g'(\eta) < 0$. Hence, when the cost of communication declines, E comes into the economy.

4.3 Summary and Insights

With the benefits of ICT-enabled communication networks, decline in cost of communication, and utilization of TZ differences, it is interesting to know the impact on skilled and unskilled workers and sectoral composition. The spread of such technology and its utilization translates into enhanced productivity growth. International transactions via e-commerce and mobility of human capital-induced skill as well as physical capital are conducive to utilization of state-of-the-art technologies like ICT and its concomitant effects on welfare and gains from trade (Marjit, Mandal and Nakanishi [2020]). It is shown that both types of worker gain, although skilled workers accrual more gains. Moreover, use of educational capital leading to skill acquisition guarantees a rise in output of the skilled-intensive sector, but at the expense of wage inequality, that is, widening the gap between skilled and unskilled labor. Sourcing of educational capital also matters for complementarity among sectors. Overall, gains occur with increase in trade volume.

5 Conclusion and Road Ahead

"You may delay, but time will not."

Benjamin Franklin

Despite being a nonrenewable resource, time has not been given due importance in economics except in a few areas (see, for example, Becker [1965]). International economics, where trade occurs between nations that are located geographically apart, is one such area. To the best of our knowledge, Roy (2005) is one that considered in the Beckerian framework the role of *ability differences* for time allocation to generate trade in goods, without consideration of *time differences* for fragmenting production over stages. In this Element, we have developed a framework – novel in its approach, unique in terms of its dealing with international trade taking place on virtual platforms – and contributed toward incorporating the time dimension in the trade literature. The word "virtual" at first glance refers to something unreal since we cannot touch or feel such object. However, this has become more "real" than anything around us. It is this reality – within an invisible realm – that we have tried to capture in terms of simple economics. In reality, most countries are situated in different TZs (overlapping or nonoverlapping), although there are countries, such as South Korea and Japan, that are located in identically overlapping TZs. Quite obviously, the time dimension plays a crucial role in opening the door to engage over virtual networks. Breakthroughs in ICT enable bridging the time difference in a conducive way.

Virtual markets roughly represent exchange of goods and services via virtual platforms. In this Element, we have discussed virtual markets, emphasizing cross-border transactions in terms of ICT-driven business process outsourcing between nations located in mostly NOLTZs. This being a source of natural comparative advantage to generate exchanges between them is quite intuitive, yet vastly ignored in the domain of international trade literature. Although some empirical works emphasizing this kind of new TZ-based natural comparative advantage exist, theoretical literature capturing the essential mechanism is almost nonexistent. Clearly, Kikuchi (2011) and Marjit (2007) are the precursors in this challenging but fertile research area. This culminated into a monograph emphasizing the fourth dimension of trade – trade based on TZ differences as opposed to factor endowments and productivity differences – in Marjit, Mandal and Nakanishi (2020). The preceding sections overviewed the traditional literature, identified the lacunae in trade theory, pointed out the point of departure from modern theories of trade, and gradually developed models incorporating aspects of international trade in intermediate services occurring virtually between nations, thanks to the ICT revolution. Although we have systematically explored the importance of such trade and issues of productivity, sustained growth, human capital and wage inequality in theoretical models, many issues remain unearthed and those need further investigation.

It is clear by now that physical or spatial demarcations of economic activities become truly meaningless in a world that is seamlessly connected virtually. Thus, the most fundamental problem that bothers policymakers has to do with the regulation of such markets and, hence, trade policy in a separated, TZ-driven world would be a good topic for research in years to come. As all these occur in virtual platforms, issues related to policies to ensure privacy of information, protection of data, and so on require global cooperation. These are gaining attention in recent works (see, for example, Grossman, McCalman and Staiger [2021] and McCalman [2021, 2022]).

In a way, free trade and exchange are natural consequences of a virtual world. It is extremely difficult to impose a tariff on virtual imports unless such virtual transactions need a critical physical transaction somewhere in the supply chain. It is this mix and match of virtual and real that should draw the attention of researchers in future. How to design cyber regulations in the face of negative externalities (for example, cybercrime or fraudulent practices) or for controlling transactions that are harmful will continue to be a matter of great concern to policymakers for many years to come. This will call for more research in this area. While technology used to check fraudulent practices in virtual trading in financial markets is a good example, it is the design of economic transactions that needs to be examined.

An interesting emerging area seems to be the economics of crypto or virtual currencies. This requires the formulation of independent monetary policy of sovereign nations when money supply includes a completely unregulated component generated via machines or AI. Bypassing government rules and regulations will be much easier in a situation with greater trust on virtual currencies as a medium of exchange, and store of value. However, chaotic disruptions in global trading and financial systems cannot be ruled out and that is the challenge to researchers and policymakers.

One critical question should be whether virtual markets help or hurt employment. We need to look at substitution and volume effects from a new perspective. Technological change, wherever it strikes, will always have these two effects. It tends to make some of the existing inputs, including traditional human capital, obsolete; for example, manual typists have vanished with the introduction of personal computers. But growth in terms of larger volumes of production is likely to increase demand for new types of worker, creating incentives for training and learning. Eventually it may possibly raise inequality. More work in this area is essential.

We have elaborated in the text on the idea that the role of time in determining patterns of trade through virtual interaction across NOLTZs must be taken into account to appreciate new aspects of international trade. Another way time enters the picture is through trade *between* rich and poor countries in terms of virtual and nonvirtual transactions. Richer countries have greater opportunity costs of time and, therefore, are willing to spend more, other things being equal, to avoid physical transactions. Therefore, under autarky, virtual goods would be relatively expensive in these countries and they would import virtual goods. In a way, nonvirtual transactions would be more valuable in poorer countries as relative cost of time is less there. This point has been theorized in Marjit and Yang (2021). Also *within* a country, richer groups would want to hire the services of poorer groups for time-intensive work for the same reason that the poor may have lower opportunity cost of time. This aspect is dealt with in Marjit, Pant and Huria (2020).

Call centers in developing countries cater to the needs of developed country customers by providing assistance with respect to various kinds of services. Such call centers actually operate during the night in countries such as India, in contrast with BPO models with separated TZs as analyzed in Marjit, Mandal and Nakanishi (2020), Nakanishi and Long (2015) and related literature. This might be the case where nighttime jobs in the poor countries or daytime jobs in the rich countries are up for grabs through virtual platforms and workers do not have to move physically. But this does not answer the question of why, for similar needs as in India, call centers do not open in the USA. That has to do with the fact that US workers prefer working during the daytime because of greater job opportunities in regular hours, thus making relative labor supply at night lower in the USA and very expensive, which Indians may not like to afford. Thus, the opportunity cost of time is a serious deciding factor in any type of VT.

Close on the heels of this issue is the idea of whether face-to-face interactions are necessary in virtual transactions, that is, whether similar (or overlapping) TZs need to be used between agents for more productive interactions of some kind. That will reduce the criticality of separated (or nonoverlapping) TZs for VT.

Trade with time as a catalyst alters the notion of "distance" as usually used in trade theory over centuries and translates into voluminous work on gravity models. As mentioned throughout the text, contrary to the conventional empirical trade models using specifications of gravity models, here longer spatial distance can actually promote VT because countries can work along separated TZs, and timely delivery is conducive for promoting trade with reduction in costs of communication. In that way, distance does not necessarily deter trade. However, larger distances between countries may have been positively correlated with asymmetries in both factor endowments and knowledge, leading to greater volumes of both real and virtual trade. Probably, revisiting the gravity model and its offshoots to feature rising VT transactions overtaking the barriers of physical distance would be a step forward for empirical research grounded on the theories presented in this Element. Then, probably the role of time as truly causing the death of distance would come into the limelight. All such issues should feature in future work on the subject.

References

Acemoglu, D. (2009). *Introduction to Modern Economic Growth*. Princeton, NJ: Princeton University Press.

Acemoglu, D., and Azar, P. D. (2020). Endogenous production networks. *Econometrica*, **88**(1), 33–82.

Acemoglu, D., Ozdaglar, A. E., and Tahbaz-Salehi, A. (2010). Cascades in Networks and Aggregate Volatility. NBER Working Paper w1516. Cambridge, MA: National Burea of Economic Research. https://ssrn.com/abstract=1703309.

Acemoglu, D., and Ventura, J. (2002). The world income distribution. *Quarterly Journal of Economics*, **117**(2), 659–694.

Acharyya, R., and Kar, S. (2013). *International Trade and Economic Development*. Oxford: Oxford University Press.

Acharyya, R., and Marjit, S., eds. (2014). *Trade, Globalization and Development: Essays in Honour of Kalyan K. Sanyal*. New Delhi: Springer India.

Aghion, P., Antonin, C., and Bunel, S. (2021). *The Power of Creative Destruction: Economic Upheaval and the Wealth of Nations*. Cambridge, MA: Harvard University Press.

Aghion, P., and Durlauf, S. N. (2005). *Handbook of Economic Growth*, vols. I and II. Amsterdam: Elsevier.

Aghion, P., and Howitt, P. W. (2008). *The Economics of Growth*. Cambridge, MA: MIT Press.

Alesina, A., Spolaore, E., and Wacziarg, R. (2005). Trade, growth and the size of countries. In P. Aghion and S. N. Durlauf, eds., *Handbook of Economic Growth*, vol. 1B, 1499–1542. Amsterdam: Elsevier.

Anderson, E. (2000). Why do nations trade (so little)? *Pacific Economic Review*, **5**(2), 115–134.

(2014). Time differences, communication and trade: Longitude matters II. *Review of World Economics*, **150**(2), 337–369.

Anderson, J. E., and van Wincoop, E. (2004). Trade costs. *Journal of Economic Literature*, **42**(3), 691–751.

Antràs, P. (2003). Firms, contracts and trade structure. *Quarterly Journal of Economics*, **118**(4), 1375–1418.

Antràs, P., Chor, D., Fally, T., and Hillberry, R. (2012). Measuring the upstreamness of production and trade flows. *American Economic Review*, **102**(3), 412–416.

Antràs, P., and Gortari, A. D. (2020). On the geography of global value chains. *Econometrica*, **88**(4), 1553–1598.

Antràs, P., and Helpman, E. (2004). Global sourcing. *Journal of Political Economy*, **112**(3), 552–580.

Autor, D., Katz, L. F., and Krueger, A. B. (1998). Computing inequality: Have computers changed the labor market? *Quarterly Journal of Economics*, **113**(4), 1169–1213.

Bahar, D. (2020). The hardships of long-distance relationships: Time zone proximity and the location of MNC's knowledge-intensive activities. *Journal of International Economics*, **125**, 103311.

Baldwin, R. (2016). *The Great Convergence*. Cambridge, MA: Harvard University Press.

Baldwin, R., and Dingel, J. I. (2021). Telemigration and Development: On the Offshorability of Teleworkable Jobs. NBER Working Paper No. 29387. Cambridge, MA: National Bureau of Economic Research.

Bardhan, P. (2003). *Essays in International Trade, Growth and Development*. Oxford: Basil Blackwell.

Barro, R. J., and Sala-i-Martin, X. (1995). *Economic Growth*. New York: McGraw-Hill International Edition.

Becker, G. S. (1965). A theory of the allocation of time. *Economic Journal*, **75** (299), 493–517.

Beladi, H., Jones, R. W., and Marjit, S. (1997). Technology for sale. *Pacific Economic Review*, **2**(3), 187–196.

Beladi, H., Marjit, S., and Weiher, K. (2011). An analysis of the demand for skill in a growing economy. *Economic Modelling*, **28**(4), 1471–1474.

Berman, E., Bound, J., and Machin, S. (1998). Implications of skill-biased technological change: International evidence. *Quarterly Journal of Economics*, **CXIII**(4), 1245–1279.

Bernard, A. B., Eaton, J., Jensen, J. B., and Kortum, S. (2003). Plants and productivity in international trade. *American Economic Review*, **93**(4), 1268–1290.

Bernard, A. B., Jensen, J. B., and Schott, P. K. (2006). Trade costs, firms and productivity. *Journal of Monetary Economics*, **53**(5), 917–937.

Bhagwati, J., and Dehejia, V. H. (1994). Freer trade and wages of the unskilled: Is Marx striking again? In J. Bhagwati and M. H. Kosters, eds., *Trade and Wages: Leveling Wages Down?* 37–75. Washington, DC: AEI Press.

Blum, B. S. (2008). Trade, technology, and the rise of the service sector: The effects on US wage inequality. *Journal of International Economics*, **74**, 441–458.

Bonadio, B., Huo, Z., Levchenko, A. A., and Pandalai-Nayar, N. (2021). Global supply chains in the pandemic. *Journal of International Economics*, **133**, 103534.

Borchert, I., and Yotov, Y. V. (2017). Distance, globalization and international trade. *Economics Letters*, **153**(C), 32–38.

Brander, J., and Krugman, P. (1983). A "reciprocal dumping" model of international trade. *Journal of International Economics*, **15**(3–4), 313–321.

Brynjolfsson, E., and McAfee, A. (2014). *The Second Machine Age: Work, Progress, and Prosperity in a Time of Brilliant Technologies*. New York: W. W. Norton and Company.

Bucchholz, T. G. (2007). *New Ideas from Dead Economists: An Introduction to Modern Economic Thought*. New York: Penguin.

Buera, F. J., and Lucas, R. E. (2018). Idea flows and economic growth. *Annual Review of Economics*, **10**(1), 315–345.

Buera, F. J., and Oberfield, E. (2020). The global diffusion of ideas. *Econometrica*, **88**(1), 83–114.

Cassing, J. H. (1978). Transport costs in international trade theory: A comparison with the analysis of non-traded goods. *Quarterly Journal of Economics*, **92**(4), 535–550.

Catão, L., and Obstfeld, M. (2019). *Meeting Globalization's Challenges: Policies to Make Trade Work for All*. Princeton, NJ: Princeton University Press.

Caves, R. E., Frankel, J. A., and Jones, R. W. (2007). *World Trade and Payments: An Introduction*, 6th ed. New York: Harper Collins.

Chakrabarti, A. (2004). Asymmetric adjustment costs in simple general equilibrium models. *European Economic Review*, **48**, 63–73.

Chaney, T. (2011). The Network Structure of International Trade. NBER Working Paper 16753. Cambridge, MA: National Bureau of Economic Research.

Choi, E. K., and Choi, J. Y. (2013). Financial advantage, outsourcing and FDI under wage uncertainty. *North American Journal of Economics and Finance*, **24**, 260–267.

Chusseau, N., Dumont, M., and Hellier, J. (2008). Explaining rising inequality: Skill-biased technical change and north–south trade. *Journal of Economic Surveys*, **22**(3), 409–457.

Coe, D. T., and Helpman, E. (1995). International R&D spillovers. *European Economic Review*, **39**, 859–887.

Coe, D. T., Helpman, E., and Hoffmaister, A. W. (1997). North–South R&D spillovers. *Economic Journal*, **107**, 134–149.

Crafts, N. F. R. (1973). Trade as a handmaiden of growth: An alternative view. *Economic Journal*, **83**(331), 875–884.

Cravino, J., and Sotelo, S. (2019). Trade-induced structural change and the skill premium. *American Economic Journal: Macroeconomics*, **11**(3), 289–326.

Das, G. G. (2002). Trade, technology and human capital: Stylized facts and quantitative evidence. *World Economy*, **25**(2), 257–281.

(2007). Who leads and who lags? Technology diffusion, e-commerce and trade facilitation in a model of Northern hub vis-à-vis Southern spokes. *Journal of Economic Integration*, **22**(4), 929–972.

(2015). Why some countries are slow in acquiring new technologies? A model of trade-led diffusion and absorption. *Journal of Policy Modeling*, **37**(1), 65–91.

Das, G. G., and Drine, I. (2020). Distance from the technology frontier: How could Africa catch-up via socio-institutional factors and human capital? *Technological Forecasting and Social Change*, **150**(C), 119755.

Das, G. G., and Han, H. (2013). Trade in middle products between South Korea and China: A survey on the extent of offshore production-sharing. In A. Bardhan, D. M. Jaffee and C. A. Kroll, eds., *The Oxford Handbook of Offshoring and Global Employment*, 276–310. Oxford: Oxford University Press.

Davis, D. (1998). Technology, unemployment and relative wages in a global economy. *European Economic Review*, **42**(9), 1613–1633.

Deardorff, A. V. (2003). Time and trade: The role of time in determining the structure and effects of international trade, with an application to Japan. In R. M. Stern, ed., *Japan's Economic Recovery*, 63–76. Cheltenham: Edward Elgar.

(2004). Local Comparative Advantage: Trade Costs and the Pattern of Trade. DP No. 500, University of Michigan. https://EconPapers.repec.org/RePEc: mie:wpaper:500.

Dettmer, B. (2014). International service transactions: Is time a trade barrier in a connected world? *International Economic Journal*, **28**(2), 225–254.

Dixit, A. K., and Grossman, G. M. (1982). Trade and protection with multistage production. *Review of Economic Studies*, **49**, 583–94.

Dixit, A. K., and Stiglitz, J. E. (1977). Monopolistic competition and optimum product diversity. *American Economic Review*, **67**, 297–308.

Do, V., and Long, N. V. (2008). International outsourcing under monopolistic competition: Winners and losers. In S. Marjit and E. S. H. Yu, eds., *Contemporary and Emerging Issues in Trade Theory and Policy*, 345–366. Bingley: Emerald Group.

Dollar, D. (1992). Outward-oriented developing economies really do grow more rapidly: Evidence from 95 LDCs, 1976–1985. *Economic Development and Cultural Change*, **40**(3), 523–544.

Dorn, F., F., Clemens, P., and Niklas (2021). Trade Openness and Income Inequality: New Empirical Evidence. CESifo Working Paper 9203. http://dx.doi.org/10.2139/ssrn.3892627.

Dornbusch, R., Fischer, S., and Samuelson, P. A. (1977). Comparative advantage, trade, and payments in a Ricardian model with a continuum of goods. *American Economic Review*, **67**(5), 823–839.

Dreher, A., and Gaston, N. (2008). Has globalization increased inequality? *Review of International Economics*, **16**(3), 516–536.

Duernecker, G., Meyer, M., Vega-Redondo, F. (2021). Trade Openness and Growth: A Network- Based Approach. CESifo Working Paper 9319.

Eaton, J., and Kortum, S. (1999). International technology diffusion: Theory and measurement. *International Economic Review*, **40**(3), 537–570.

  (2012). Putting Ricardo to work. *Journal of Economic Perspectives*, **26**(2), 65–90.

Eels, F. R. (1956). The economics of shift working. *Journal of Industrial Economics*, **5**, 51–62.

Egger, P. H., and Larch, M. (2013). Time zone differences as trade barriers. *Economics Letters*, **119**, 172–175.

Falvey, R. E. (1976). Transport costs in the pure theory of international trade. *Economic Journal*, **86**(343), 536–550.

Feenstra, R. (1998). Integration of trade and disintegration of production in the global economy. *Journal of Economic Perspectives*, **12**(4), 31–50.

  (2004). *Advanced International Trade: Theory and Evidence*. Princeton, NJ: Princeton University Press.

  (2010). *Offshoring in the Global Economy: Microeconomic Structure and Macroeconomic Implications*. Cambridge, MA: MIT Press.

Feenstra, R. C., and Hanson, G. H. (1996). Globalization, Outsourcing and Wage Inequality. NBER Working Paper 5424. Cambridge, MA: National Bureau of Economic Research.

Feenstra, R., and Taylor, A. (2021). *International Economics*, 4th ed. New York: Worth Publishers.

Findlay, R. (1974). Relative prices, growth and trade in a simple Ricardian system. *Economica*, **41**(161), 1–13.

  (1978). An "Austrian" model of international trade and interest rate equalization. *Journal of Political Economy*, **86**, 989–1007.

(1984). Growth and development in trade models. In R. W. Jones and P. B. Kenen, eds., *Handbook of International Economics*, vol. 1, 185–236. Amsterdam: Elsevier.

(1995). Infrastructure, human capital and international trade. *Swiss Journal of Economics and Statistics (SJES)*, **131**(III), 289–301.

Frankel, J. A. (1997). *Regional Trading Blocs in the World Trading System*. Washington, DC: Institute of International Economics.

Frankel, J. A., and Romer, D. H. (1999). Does trade cause growth? *American Economic Review*, **89**(3), 379–399.

Furusawa, T., Konishi, H., and Anh Tran, D. L. (2019). International trade and income inequality. *Scandinavian Journal of Economics*, **122**(3), 993–1026.

Goldberg, P. K., Khandelwal, A. K., Pavcnik, N., and Topalova, P. (2010a). Imported intermediate inputs and domestic product growth: Evidence from India. *Quarterly Journal of Economics*, **125**(4), 1727–1767.

(2010b). Multiproduct firms and product turnover in the developing world: Evidence from India. *Review of Economics and Statistics*, **92**(4), 1042–1049.

Grossman, G. M., and Helpman, E. (1990). Trade, innovation, and growth. *American Economic Review*, **80**(2), 86–91.

(1991a). Trade, knowledge spillovers, and growth. *European Economic Review*, **35**(2–3), 517–526.

(1991b). *Innovation and Growth in the Global Economy*. Cambridge, MA: MIT Press.

Grossman, G. M., McCalman, P., and Staiger, R. W. (2021). The "new" economics of trade agreements: From trade liberalization to regulatory convergence? *Econometrica*, **89**(1), 215–249.

Grossman, G. M., and Rogoff, K. (2005). *Handbook of International Economics*, vol. 3. Amsterdam: North-Holland.

Grossman, G. M., and Rossi-Hansberg, E. (2008). Trade in tasks: A simple theory of offshoring. *American Economic Review*, **98**, 1978–1997.

Hamermesh, D. S. (1999). The timing of work over time. *Economic Journal*, **109**, 37–66.

Hanson, G. H. (2012). The rise of middle kingdoms: Emerging economies in global trade. *Journal of Economic Perspectives*, **26**(2), 41–64.

Harrigan, J., and Venables, A. J. (2006). Timeliness and agglomeration. *Journal of Urban Economics*, **59**, 300–316.

Harris, R. G. (1998). The Internet as a GPT: Factor market implications. In E. Helpman, ed., *General Purpose Technologies and Economic Growth*, 145–166. Cambridge, MA: MIT Press.

Haskel, J., Lawrence, R. Z., Leamer, E. E., and Slaughter, M. J. (2012). Globalization and U.S. wages: Modifying classic theory to explain recent facts. *Journal of Economic Perspectives*, **26**(2), 119–140.

Hattari, R., and Rajan, R. S. (2008). Sources of FDI Flows to Developing Asia: The Roles of Distance and Time Zones. ADBI Working Paper 117. Tokyo: Asian Development Bank Institute.

Head, K., and Mayer, T. (2014). Gravity equations: Workhorse, toolkit, and cookbook. In G. Gopinath, E. Helpman and K. Rogogg, eds., *Handbook of International Economics*, vol. 4, 131–195. Amsterdam: Elsevier.

Head, K., Mayer, T., and Ries, J. (2009). How remote is the offshoring threat? *European Economic Review*, **53**, 429–444.

Heckscher, E. (1919). The effect of foreign trade on the distribution of income. *Ekonomisk Tidskrift*, **21**, 497–512. Reprinted as chapter 13 in American Economic Association (1949). Readings in the Theory of International Trade, 272–300. Homewood, IL: Richard D. Irwin.

Helpman, E. (1981). International trade in the presence of product differentiation, economies of scale and monopolistic competition: A Chamberlin-Heckscher-Ohlin approach. *Journal of International Economics*, 11(3), 305–340.

(2004). *The Mystery of Economic Growth*. Cambridge, MA: Harvard University Press.

(2011). *Understanding Global Trade*. Cambridge, MA: Harvard University Press.

Helpman, E., Itskhoki, O., Muendler, M., and Redding, S. (2012). Trade and Inequality: From Theory to Estimation. NBER Working Paper 17991. Cambridge, MA: National Bureau of Economic Research.

Helpman, E., and Krugman, P. (1987). *Market Structure and Foreign Trade: Increasing Returns, Imperfect Competition and the International Economy*. Cambridge, MA: MIT Press.

Hicks, J. (1973). *Capital and Time: A Neo-Austrian Theory*. London: Oxford Calendar Press.

Hidalgo, C. (2015). *Why Information Grows: The Evolution of Order, from Atoms to Economies*. New York: Basic Books.

Hummels, D. L., and Schaur, G. (2013). Time as a trade barrier. *American Economic Review*, **103**(7), 2935–2959.

Iacovone, L., Rauch, F., and Winters, L. A. (2013). Trade as an engine of creative destruction: Mexican experience with Chinese competition. *Journal of International Economics*, **89**(2), 379–392.

Irwin, D. (1996). *Against the Tide: An Intellectual History of Free Trade*. Princeton, NJ: Princeton University Press.

Jones, C. I. (2016). The facts of economic growth. In J. B. Taylor and H. Uhlig, eds., *Handbook of Macroeconomics*, vol. 2A, 3–69. Amsterdam: Elsevier.

Jones, R. W. (1965). The structure of simple general equilibrium models. *Journal of Political Economy*, **73**(6), 557–572.

(1971). A three-factor model in theory, trade and history. In J. Bhagwati, R. W. Jones, R. A. Mundell and J. Vanek, eds., *Trade, Balance of Payments and Growth*, 3–21. Amsterdam: North-Holland.

(2000). *Globalization and the Theory of Input Trade*. Cambridge, MA: MIT Press.

(2018). *International Trade Theory and Competitive Models*. Singapore: World Scientific Publishers.

Jones, R. W., Beladi, H., and Marjit, S. (1999). The three faces of factor intensities. *Journal of Economics*, **48**(2), 413–420.

Jones, R. W., and Kierzkowski, H. (1990). The role of services in production and international trade: A theoretical framework. In R. W. Jones and A. Krueger, eds., *The Political Economy of International Trade*, 31–48. Oxford: Blackwell.

(2001) A framework for fragmentation. In S. W. Arndt and H. Kierzkowski, eds., *Fragmentation: New Production Patterns in the World Economy*, 17–34. Oxford: Oxford University Press.

Jones, R. W., and Marjit, S. (2001). The role of international fragmentation in the development process. *American Economic Review*, **91**, 363–366.

(1995). Labor-market aspects of enclave-led growth. *Canadian Journal of Economics*, **28**, Special Issue.

(2003). Economic development, trade and wages. *German Economic Review*, **4**(1), 1–17.

Keller, W. (2000). Do trade patterns and technology flows affect productivity growth? *World Bank Economic Review*, **14**(1), 17–47.

(2004). International technology diffusion. *Journal of Economic Literature*, **42**, 752–782.

Kemp, M. C., and Shimomura, K. (1999). Trade gains in chaotic equilibria. In E. K. Choi and B. S. Jensen, eds., *Economic Growth and International Trade*, 45–51. Oxford: Blackwell.

Kikuchi, T. (2006). Time zones, outsourcing and patterns of international trade. *Economics Bulletin*, **6**(15), 1–10.

(2011). *Time Zones, Communications Networks and International Trade*. Routledge Studies in the Modern World Economy. Abingdon: Routledge.

Kikuchi, T., and Iwasa, K. (2008). A Simple Model of Service Trade with Time Zone Differences. MPRA Paper 9574. University Library of Munich: Munich Personal RePEc Archive.

Kikuchi, T., and Long, N. V. (2011). Shift working and trade in labor services with time zone differences. CESifo Working Paper 3542, Category 8: Trade Policy. http://dx.doi.org/10.2139/ssrn.1915930.

Kikuchi, T., and Marjit, S. (2010). Time zones and periodic intra-industry trade. EERI Research Paper Series No. 08/2010. Brussels: Economics and Econometrics Research Institute.

(2011). Growth with time zone differences. *Economic Modelling*, **28**, 637–640.

Kikuchi, T., Marjit, S., and Mandal, B. (2013). Trade with time zone differences: Factor market implications. *Review of Development Economics*, **17** (4), 699–711.

Kohler, W. (2004a). International outsourcing and factor prices with multistage production. *Economic Journal*, **114**, C166–C185.

(2004b). Aspects of international fragmentation.*Review of International Economics*, **12**, 793–816.

Kosters, M. H. (1994). An overview of changing wage patterns in the labor market. In J. Bhagwati and M. H. Kosters, eds., *Trade and Wages: Leveling Wages Down?* 1–35. Washington, DC: AEI Press.

Kostiuk, P. F. (1990). Compensating differentials for shift work. *Journal of Political Economy*, **98**, 1054–1075.

Kravis, I. (1970). Trade as a handmaiden of growth: Similarities between the nineteenth and twentieth centuries. *Economic Journal*, **80**(320), 850–872.

Krugman, P. R. (1979). Increasing returns, monopolistic competition, and international trade. *Journal of International Economics*, **9**(4), 469–479.

(1980). Scale economies, product differentiation, and the pattern of trade. *American Economic Review*, **70**(5), 950–959.

(1983). New theories of trade among industrial countries. *American Economic Review*, **73**(2), 343–347.

(2008). Trade and wages: Reconsidered. *Brookings Papers on Economic Activity*, **Spring**, 103–154.

Krugman, P., and Lawrence, R. Z. (1994). Trade, jobs and wages. *Scientific American*, **270**(4), 44–49.

Krugman, P. R., Obstfeld, M., and Melitz, M. J. (2018). *International Economics: Theory and Policy*, 11th ed. Global Edition. Harlow, UK: Pearson.

Kurokawa, Y. (2012). A survey of trade and wage inequality: Anomalies, resolutions and new trends. *Journal of Economic Surveys*, **18**(1), 169–193.

Lanfranchi, J., Ohlsson, H., and Skalli, A. (2002). Compensating wage differentials and shift work preferences. *Economics Letters*, **74**, 393–398.

Limao, N., and Venables, A. (2001). Infrastructure, geographical disadvantage, transports costs and trade. *World Bank Economic Review*, **15**(3), 451–479.

Long, N. V., Riezman, R., and Soubeyran, A. (2005). Fragmentation and services. *North American Journal of Economics and Finance*, **16**, 137–152.

Lucas, R. E. (1988). On the mechanics of economic development. *Journal of Monetary Economics*, **22**(1), 3–42.

(1995). Understanding business cycles. In S. Estrin and A. Marin, eds., *Essential Readings in Economics*, 306–327. Houndmills, UK: Macmillan.

(2002). *Lectures on Economic Growth*. Cambridge, MA: Harvard University Press.

(2003). *Lectures on Economic Growth*. New Delhi: Oxford University Press.

(2009a). Ideas and growth. *Economics*, **76**, 1–19.

(2009b). Trade and the diffusion of industrial revolution. *American Economic Journal: Macroeconomics*, **1**, 1–25.

Lucas, R. E., and Moll, B. (2014). Knowledge growth and the allocation of time. *Journal of Political Economy*, **122**, 1–51.

Malgouyres, C., Mayer, T., and Mazet-Sonilhac, C. (2021). Technology-induced trade shocks? Evidence from broadband expansion in France. *Journal of International Economics*, **133**(C), 103520.

Mandal, B. (2015). Distance, production, virtual trade and growth. *Economics – The Open-Access, Open-Assessment E-Journal*, **9**(1), 1–12.

Mandal, B., Marjit, S., and Nakanishi, N. (2015). Outsourcing, Factor Prices and Skill Formation in Countries with Non-overlapping Time Zones. MPRA Paper 68227. University Library of Munich: Munich Personal RePEc Archive.

Marjit, S. (1987). Trade in intermediates and the colonial pattern of trade. *Economica*, **54**, 173–184.

(2007). Trade theory and the role of time zones. *International Review of Economics and Finance*, **16**, 153–160.

(2008). *International Trade and Economic Development: Essays in Theory and Policy*. New Delhi: Oxford University Press.

Marjit, S., and Acharyya, R. (2006). Trade liberalization, skill-linked intermediate and two-sided wage gap. *Journal of Policy Reform*, **9**(3), 203–217.

Marjit, S., and Das, G. G. (2021). Contact-Intensity, Collapsing Entertainment Sector and Wage Inequality: A Finite Change Model of COVID-19 Impact. CESifo Working Paper 9311. http://dx.doi.org/10.2139/ssrn.3932019.

Marjit, S., and Kar, S. (2009). A contemporary perspective on the informal labour market: Theory, policy and the Indian experience. *Economic and Political Weekly*, **44**(14), 60–71.

(2013). International capital flow, vanishing industries and two-sided wage inequality. *Pacific Economic Review*, **18**(5), 574–583.

eds. (2018). *International Trade, Welfare, and the Theory of General Equilibrium*. Cambridge: Cambridge University Press.

Marjit, S., and Mandal, B. (2012). Domestic trading costs and pure theory of international trade. *International Journal of Economic Theory*, **8**(2), 165–178.

(2017). Virtual trade between separated time zones and growth. *International Journal of Economic Theory*, **13**(2), 171–183.

Marjit, S., Mandal, B., and Nakanishi, N. (2020). *Virtual Trade and Comparative Advantage: The Fourth Dimension*. Singapore: Springer.

Marjit, S., Pant, M., and Huria, S. (2020). Unskilled immigration, technical progress, and wages: Role of the household sector. *Review of International Economics*, **28**(1), 235–251.

Marjit, S., and Yang, L. (2021). An Elementary Theorem on Gains from Virtual Trade. CESifo Working Paper 8703. http://dx.doi.org/10.2139/ssrn .3736485.

Markusen, J. R. (2021). Ronald Jones's duality analysis as a foundation for applied general-equilibrium modeling. *International Journal of Economic Theory*, **17**(1), 6–19.

Matsuoka, Y., and Fukushima, M. (2010). Time zones, shift working and international outsourcing. *International Review of Economics and Finance*, **19**, 769–778.

McCalman, P. (2021). Trade Policy with FANG's (aka Trade Policy and Multi-sided Platforms). Working Paper, https://drive.google.com/file/d/ 1o740qKVo7dPpDyPM1_3xMmMLeZFs6GAt/view.

(2022). e-Globalization and Trade Agreements. Working Paper, https://drive .google.com/file/d/1skUk6cYhj5ejmEJySyHderLh_1Xa-vxt/view.

Melitz, M. J. (2003). The impact of trade on intra-industry reallocation and aggregate industry productivity. *Econometrica*, **71**(6), 1695–1725.

Melitz, M., and Ottaviano, G. (2005). Market Size, Trade, and Productivity. NBER Working Paper 11393. Cambridge, MA: National Bureau of Economic Research.

Melitz, M. J., and Redding, S. (2012). Heterogeneous Firms and Trade. NBER Working Paper 18652. Cambridge, MA: National Bureau of Economic Research.

(2021). Trade and Innovation. CEPR Discussion Paper 16264. https://cepr .org/publications/dp16264.

Melitz, M. J., and Trefler, D. (2012). Gains from trade when firms matter. *Journal of Economic Perspectives*, **26**(2), 91–118.

Morton, F. S. (2006). Consumer benefit from use of the Internet. In A. B. Jaffe, J. Lerner, and S. Stern, eds., *Innovation Policy and the Economy*, vol. 6. National Bureau of Economic Research, 67–90. Cambridge, MA: MIT Press.

Nakanishi, N., and Long, N. V. (2015). The distributional and allocative impacts of virtual labor mobility across time zones through communication networks. *Review of International Economics*, **23**(3), 638–662.

Navaretti, G. B., and Tarr, D. (2000). International knowledge flows and economic performance: A review of the evidence. *World Bank Economic Review*, **14**(1), 1–15.

Ohlin, B. (1933). *Inter-regional and International Trade*. Cambridge, MA: Harvard University Press.

Osnago, A., and Tan, S. W. (2016). Disaggregating the Impact of the Internet on International Trade. World Bank Policy Research Working Paper 7785. Washington, DC: World Bank.

Pavcnik, N. (2019). International trade and inequality in developing economies: Assessing the recent evidence. In L. A. V. Catão and M. Obstfeld, eds., *Meeting Globalization's Challenges: Policies to Make Trade Work for All*, 129–142. Princeton, NJ: Princeton University Press.

Porter, M. E. (1985). *The Competitive Advantage: Creating and Sustaining Superior Performance*. New York: Free Press.

Posner, R. A. (1973). *Economic Analysis of Law*. Boston, MA: Little, Brown and Co.

Ricardo, D. ([1817] 1951).On the principles of political economy and taxation. In P. Sraffa, ed., The Works and Correspondence of David Ricardo, vol. 1. Cambridge: Cambridge University Press, 1951.

Richardson, J. D. (1995). Income inequality and trade: How to think, what to conclude. *Journal of Economic Perspectives*, **9**, 33–55.

Rivera-Batiz, L., and Romer, P. (1991). Economic integration and endogenous growth. *Quarterly Journal of Economics*, **106**(2), 531–555.

Robertson, R. (2003). *The Three Waves of Globalization: A History of Developing Global Consciousness*. New York: Zed Books.

Rodriguez, F., and Rodrik, D. (2001). Trade policy and economic growth: A skeptic's guide to the cross-national evidence. In B. S. Bernanke and K. Rogoff, eds., *NBER Macroeconomics Annual 2000*, vol. 15, 261–338. Cambridge, MA: MIT Press.

Rodrik, D. (2007). *One Economics, Many Recipes: Globalization, Institutions, and Economic Growth*. Princeton, NJ: Princeton University Press.

(2017). *Straight Talk on Trade: Ideas for a Sane World Economy*. Princeton, NJ: Princeton University Press.

(2021). A Primer on Trade and Inequality. NBER Working Paper 29507. Cambridge, MA: National Bureau of Economic Research.

Rodrik, D., Subramanian, A., and Tebbi, F. (2002). Institutions Rule: The Primacy of Institutions over Geography and Integration in Economic Development. NBER Working Paper 9305. Cambridge, MA: National Bureau of Economic Research.

Romer, P. M. (1990). Endogenous technological change. *Journal of Political Economy*, **98**(5), S71–S102.

(1994). New goods, old theory, and the welfare costs of trade restrictions. *Journal of Development Economics*, **43**(1), 5–38.

Roy, U. (2005). International trade and the value of time. *Review of International Economics*, **13**(4),757–769.

Ruffin, R. J., and Jones, R. W. (2007) International technology transfer: Who gains and who loses? *Review of International Economics*, **15**(2), 209–222.

Sachs, J. D., and Shatz, H. (1996). U.S. trade with developing countries and wage inequality. *American Economic Review*, **86**(2), 234–239.

Sachs, J. D., and Warner, A. M. (1995). Economic reform and the process of global integration. Brookings Papers on Economic Activity 1–118. http://dx.doi.org/10.2307/2534573.

Sala-i-Martin, X. (1997). I just ran two million regressions. *American Economic Review*, **87**(2), 178–183.

Samuelson, P. A. (1971). Ohlin was right. *Swedish Journal of Economics*, **73**(4), 365–384.

Sanyal, K. (1983). Vertical specialization in a Ricardian model with a continuum of stages of production. *Economica*, **50**(197), 71–78.

Sanyal, K., and Jones, R. W. (1982). The theory of trade in middle products. *American Economic Review*, **72**(1), 16–31.

Sarkar, A. (1985). A model of trade in intermediate goods. *Journal of International Economics*, **19**(1–2), 85–98.

Sen, A. (1960). *Growth Economics*. Harmondsworth: Penguin Books.

Singh, N., and Marjit, S., eds. (2003). *Joint Ventures, International Investment and Technology Transfer*. New York: Oxford University Press.

Sleuwaegen, L., and Smith, P. M. (2021). Service characteristics and the choice between exports and FDI: Evidence from Belgian firms. *International Economics*, **168**, 115–131.

Smith, A. ([1776] 1976). An Inquiry into the Nature and Causes of the Wealth of Nations, ed. E. Cannan, vol. 1. Chicago, IL: University of Chicago Press (originally published in 1904 by Methuen).

Solow, R. M. (2000). *Growth Theory: An Exposition*, 2nd ed. New York: Oxford University Press.

Sridhar, V. (2019). *Emerging ICT Policies and Regulations: Roadmap to Digital Economies*. Singapore: Springer.

Stein, E., and Daude, C. (2007). Longitude matters: Time zones and the location of foreign direct investment. *Journal of International Economics*, **71**(1), 96–112.

Stiglitz, J. E., and Charlton, A. (2007). *Fair Trade for All: How Trade Can Promote Development*. New York: Oxford University Press.

Stiglitz, J., and Greenwald, B. (2014). *Creating a Learning Society: A New Approach to Growth, Development, and Social Progress*. New York: Columbia University Press.

Sun, M. (2021). The Internet and SME participation in exports. *Information Economics and Policy*, **57**, 100940.

Tomasik, R. (2013). Time zone-related continuity and synchronization effects on bilateral trade flows. *Review of World Economics*, **149**, 321–342.

Ventura, J. (2005). A global view of economic growth. In P. Aghion and S. N. Durlauf, eds., *Handbook of Economic Growth*, vol. 1B, 1419–1497. Amsterdam: North-Holland.

Vernon, R. (1966). International investment and international trade in the product cycle. *Quarterly Journal of Economics*, **80**(2), 190–207.

Wang, W., Findlay, C., and Thangavelu, S. (2021). Trade, technology, and the labour market: Impacts on wage inequality within countries. *Asian-Pacific Economic Literature*, **35**(1), 19–35.

Williamson, J. G. (1998). Policy backlash: Can the past inform the present? In P. Aghion and J. G. Williamson, eds., *Growth, Inequality and Globalization: Theory, History and Policy*, 169–193. New York: Cambridge University Press.

Wood, A. (1994). *North–South Trade, Employment and Inequality: Changing Fortunes in a Skill-Driven World*. New York: Oxford University Press.

World Bank. (2001). Globalization, Growth and Poverty: Building an Inclusive World Economy. A World Bank Policy Research Report. Washington, DC: World Bank.

(2020). World Development Report: Trading for Development in the Age of Global Value Chains. Washington, DC: World Bank. doi: 10.1596/978-1-4648-1457-0.

(2021). At your Service? The Promise of Services-Led Development. (Authors G. Nayyar, M. Hallward-Driemeier and E. Davies.) Washington, DC: World Bank. doi: 10.1596/978-1-4648-1671-0.

Zaheer, S. (2000). Time zone economics and managerial work in a global economy. In P. C. Earley and H. Singh, eds., *Innovations in International Management*, 339–353. Thousand Oaks, CA: Sage.

Zeira, J. (2007). Wage inequality, technology, and trade. *Journal of Economic Theory*, **137**, 79–103.

Acknowledgments

As we benefited from interactions and feedback from many, we take this opportunity to record our sincere acknowledgments to them. We are indebted to many economists and friends for their comments on our previous and recent works related to the issue we examine here. We are deeply indebted to especially Asis Kumar Banerjee, Hamid Beladi, Eric Bond, Fumio Dei, Peter Dixon, Yunfang Hu, Ron Jones, Murray Kemp, Toru Kikuchi, Ngo Van Long, Arijit Mukherjee, Noritsugu Nakanishi, Marcel Thum, Lei Yang, Eden Yu, Lex Zhao, among others whom we could not include for reasons of parsimony but to whom we express our gratitude. We also benefited from academic visits to the University of Queensland; Australian National University; CES-Ifo Munich; the IMF (International Monetary Fund) in Washington, DC; City University of Hong Kong; the University of Nottingham, UK; Queen Mary University of London; Kobe University; University of Tokyo; Indira Gandhi Institute of Development Research, India; Soka University; and Delhi School of Economics.

This Element would not have seen the light of day without the constant encouragement and moral support of our near and dear ones. Sugata Marjit wishes to thank Baisakhi Marjit; Gouranga G. Das acknowledges Saswati Paul; and Biswajit Mandal extends a note of appreciation to Saswati Chaudhuri for their continuing support throughout this endeavor.

Our special thanks go to Kenneth Reinert and Cambridge University Press for the invitation to publish this work under Cambridge Elements in International Economics.

Cambridge Elements ⹀

International Economics

Kenneth A. Reinert

George Mason University

Kenneth A. Reinert is Professor of Public Policy in the Schar School of Policy and Government at George Mason University where he directs the Global Commerce and Policy master's degree program. He is author of *An Introduction to International Economics: New Perspectives on the World Economy* with Cambridge University Press and coauthor of *Globalization for Development: Meeting New Challenges* with Oxford University Press. He is also editor of *The Handbook of Globalisation and Development* with Edward Elgar and co-editor of the two-volume *Princeton Encyclopedia of the World Economy* with Princeton University Press.

About the Series

International economics is a distinct field with both fundamental theoretical insights and increasing empirical and policy relevance. The *Cambridge Elements in International Economics* showcases this field, covering the subfields of international trade, international money and finance, and international production, and featuring both established researchers and new contributors from all parts of the world. It aims for a level of theoretical discourse slightly above that of the *Journal of Economic Perspectives* to maintain accessibility. It extends Cambridge University Press' established reputation in international economics into the new, digital format of *Cambridge Elements*. It attempts to fill the niche once occupied by the *Princeton Essays in International Finance*, a series that no longer exists.There is a great deal of important work that takes place in international economics that is set out in highly theoretical and mathematical terms. This new Elements does not eschew this work but seeks a broader audience that includes academic economists and researchers, including those working in international organizations, such as the World Bank, the International Monetary Fund, and the Organization for Economic Cooperation and Development.

Cambridge Elements ≡

International Economics

Elements in the Series

A full series listing is available at: www.cambridge.org/CEIE